war
of words

Resources for Changing Lives

A series published in cooperation with
THE CHRISTIAN COUNSELING AND EDUCATIONAL FOUNDATION
Glenside, Pennsylvania

Susan Lutz, Series Editor

Available in the series:

war
of words

getting to the

heart of your

communication

struggles

Paul David Tripp

PUBLISHING
P.O. BOX 817 • PHILLIPSBURG • NEW JERSEY 08865-0817

With few exceptions, Scripture quotations are from the HOLY BIBLE, NEW INTERNATIONAL VERSION®. NIV®. Copyright © 1973, 1978, 1984 by International Bible Society. Used by permission of Zondervan Publishing House. All rights reserved. *Italics (or* reversed *italics) indicate emphasis added.* The exceptions are passages at the heads of chapters 3–13 and at the head of each part division, which are from *The Message* by Eugene H. Peterson (Colorado Springs: NavPress, 1993).

Prayers at the beginning of part divisions are from *Prayers for Troubled Times* by Jay E. Adams (Phillipsburg, N.J.: P&R Publishing, 1979). Used by permission.

Page design by Tobias Design
Typesetting by Michelle Feaster

Printed in the United States of America

Library of Congress Cataloging-in-Publication Data

Tripp, Paul David, 1950-
    War of words : getting to the heart of your communication struggles / Paul David Tripp.
        p. cm — (Resources for changing lives)
    Includes bibliographical references and index.
    ISBN-10: 0-87552-604-7 (pbk.)
    ISBN-13: 978-0-87552-604-1 (pbk.)
    1. Interpersonal communication—Religious aspects—Christianity.
2. Oral communication—Religious aspects—Christianity. I. Title.
II. Series.

BV4597.53.C64 T75 2000
241'.672—dc21   99-049318

To

Justin, Ethan, Nicole, and Darnay.

Jesus has used you to teach me
how to speak like the Father.
Thank you for being so patient.

Contents

Preface

WHAT makes someone write a book? Sometimes authors write because of expertise. Through education and experience they have gained a specialized knowledge and understanding of a particular topic. Their writing allows their readers to grow in the same area without undergoing all the training and experiences themselves.

An author may also write out of *desperation*. In his life there is a weakness or struggle that needs to be addressed. He examines, studies, meditates, and applies what he has learned to help himself grow. He then puts the fruit of his labors down on paper in the hope that others will benefit as he has.

I have not written this book out of expertise, but out of desperation. I have told many people during the writing process that I did not write this book, it wrote me!

When I was sixteen years old, I was rehearsing early one Saturday morning for a statewide speech competition. My mom heard me from her bedroom next door. She got up, came into the room and asked, "May I interrupt you for a moment?" I didn't really mind because I was ready to take a break. Then she said something that was nothing short of prophetic. "Paul," she said, "God has given you a special ability to communicate, but watch out, because it will also be your greatest struggle." Those words ring much truer to me today than they did the morning she spoke them.

It is true that our greatest strengths are also our greatest weaknesses. This book has been penned out of weakness—my weakness. But it is weakness that has been tempered by the intervention of God's amazing grace and the powerful insights of Scripture.

In the pages that follow, we will examine something that sets us off from the rest of creation, something we do repeatedly every day: we talk. This book, however, is different from most on the topic. It is not a discussion of the techniques and skills for effective communication. Rather, it is the story of the great battle for our hearts that is the reason for our struggle with words. Yet there is more here than just an examination of the battle. We will also get a grasp of God's plan for our talk and celebrate his enabling grace.

Thank you to all the people whose words God has used to change my heart. May God change yours as well, through the pages of this book. Thanks also to Sue Lutz, whose skill with words has made this a better book.

(part one)

talk is not cheap

Words kill, words give life;
they're either poison or fruit—
you choose. (Prov. 18:21)

That temper of mine!
   Forgive me, Lord—
   I let it get the better of me again.
When will I ever learn to wait
   until I've heard the whole story,
   to respond under pressure
   as Christ would,
   to meet evil with good?
I'm growing, Lord,
   but my growth is far too slow.
Till my life—
   break up clods of pride,
   root out weeds of selfishness,
   plow under every vestige of stubbornness.
Cultivate me and sow liberally
   more of the Spirit's
   fruit-bearing seed.
Send showers
   and storms (if need be);
   shine brightly on my soul.
Then I will sprout forth
   patience and kindness and love—
   and self-control—
   in abundance,
And my tongue will learn
   to help and heal
   and praise the Name
      of the One through Whom
      I pray,
      Amen.

Chapter One

God Speaks

And God blessed them and said to them . . .
(Gen. 1:28)

NO matter where you live, no matter what you do every day, there is one thing that you do all day long. You talk. From the first "Is it time to get up already?" to the final "Goodnight, I gotta get some sleep," you talk. In the bedroom, bathroom, hallway, and kitchen, in the car, the store, the factory, and the boardroom, you talk. To your spouse, children, friends, family, neighbors, and fellow-workers, you talk. It is what human beings do, almost without interruption and often without a thought about how important it is to human life. The ability to communicate is one of the things that separates us from the rest of creation. We are people and we talk. We need to recognize how "wordy" our lives actually are.

The word itself doesn't seem to carry the freight. "Talk" seems so normal, so ordinary, so unimportant, so harmless. Yet there are few things we do that are more important. And underneath the normality of it all is a great struggle, a war of words that we fight every day. Here are some familiar ways we talk about our struggle with words.

"I never thought when we were going together that he would talk to me the way he does now!"

"I can't believe what I'm hearing when my son talks to me!"

"She hung up on me right in the middle of a sentence."

"My parents never talk to me unless I am in trouble."

"He only talks to me nicely when he wants something."

"He talks so much it's hard to get a word in edgewise."

"I'm not comfortable with the way she talks to me about other people."

"It seems like we never have enough time to talk."

"He talked a long time, but I don't have a clue about what he was trying to say."

"Why do we always seem to end up in an argument?"

"What happened? We seemed to be so close and now we hardly ever talk."

"I feel like I spend all my time breaking up my kids' arguments!"

"Yes, he asked for my forgiveness, but I'm having a hard time letting go of the hurt. What he said was so cruel."

"I wish our family could go through an entire day without someone yelling."

"I don't know why I waste my time talking. It doesn't seem to make a bit of difference."

"We'll never get to the bottom of things if everyone keeps talking at once!"

"She always has to have the last word."

"He talks so sweetly to me when we're in public."

"Sometimes I think it would be better if we quit talking altogether."

These are all things that families have said to me in counseling. Taken together, they capture the struggle with words that all of us have. Who among us has not been hurt by the words of another? Who hasn't regretted something we ourselves have said? Who hasn't had to referee an argument? Who hasn't wanted to talk seriously with a loved one, yet there seems to be no time? Who among us can say, "My words are *always* appropriate to the situation and they are *always* kindly spoken"?

This world of talk—the world that exists behind the public calm and kindness we are all able to muster—is what this book is about. If you arc able to say, "I have no problem with my words," then you don't need to read any further. But if you recognize, like me, that there is still a war of words going on in your life, if there is still evidence of a struggle with fitting and loving communication, if there is still room for growth in your world of talk, then this book is for you.

The purpose of this book is not just to hold out the lofty standard God has set for us and then remind us how far we all fall short of it. Most of us are painfully aware of the distance between where we are and where God wants us to be. No, this book is meant to be a book of hope. It is a book about change, change that is possible because of the person and work of the Lord Jesus Christ. Jesus is the *Word* who is the only hope for *our* words! In him alone do we find victory in our own war of words.

I have written this book because I am convinced that we do not understand how radically the gospel can change the way we understand and solve our communication problems. We do not have to be discouraged! We do not have to live "stuck," and we do not have to give in to the cynicism that is such a temptation in this harsh and fallen world.

This book is a book of hope because it is rooted in four fundamental, life-altering principles:

- God has a wonderful plan for our words that is far better than any plan we could come up with on our own.
- Sin has radically altered our agenda for our words, resulting in much hurt, confusion, and chaos.
- In Christ Jesus we find the grace that provides all we need to speak as God intended us to speak.
- The Bible plainly and simply teaches us how to get from where we are to where God wants us to bc.

In every chapter of this book we will consider God's plan, our sin, his grace, and Scripture's map. My prayer is that this will lead you to a new awareness of God's design for his children, a new insight into your personal struggle with sin, a renewed reliance on God's abundant grace, and a practical biblical wisdom that results in a more God-honoring, people-benefiting life of talk.

Our Talk: The Real World

We drove through Philadelphia in silence. Finally, we had a night out with each other, yet we drove along with neither of us saying anything. It wasn't supposed to be this way. The silence was deafening and it seemed to last for hours, even though it was actually only a few minutes. In our heads we both were playing the videotape of what had happened earlier, nursing our hurt and reaffirming our innocence. Fortunately, it wasn't long before the silence was broken, forgiveness was sought and received, and we were once again enjoying rather than tolerating each other's company.

It all had started so innocently and so typically. Both of us were at the end of a long Friday at the end of a long week. Both of us had our own agenda for the evening and our own set of expectations for the other person. Both of us were more demanding than serving, and thus quickly hurt when the other rejected our ideas for the evening. Finally, both of us spoke out of that hurt. We accused rather than listened, criticized rather than looked at ourselves. Each of us gave up on the other and slid into the cocoon of our own hurt and anger.

You may be thinking, *Paul, what a depressing way to start a book that is supposed to be filled with hope!* But this mundane encounter on an unremarkable night in the Tripp family captures everything this book is about. This book is about God's wonderful plan for our words, which protects us from the pain and pressure of such moments. It is about our sin, which misdirects and distorts our words so that they are more about the desires of self than love of another. This book is about the amazing grace of the Lord that calls us back to God's purpose; grace that rescues, restores, forgives, and delivers. And this book is about simple biblical steps of repentance and change. It is about a glorious Lord who is willing and able to take our troubled worlds of talk and transform them to places where love is the motivation and peace is the result. God is at work, taking people who instinctively speak for themselves and transforming them into people who effectively speak for him.

That night, my wife Luella and I did get out of his plan for a moment, but we have learned that his grace is sufficient, that his strength is made perfect in our weakness (2 Cor. 12:9). We have seen that there is a way out. In the midst of utter personal failure, we can, by his strength, win the war of words. That is what this book is about.

Words Have Value

Words are powerful, important, significant. It was meant to be that way. When we speak, it must be with the realization that God has given our words significance. He has ordained for them to be important. Words were significant at Creation and at the Fall. They are significant to redemption. God has given words value.

He has a design for our communication, a specific plan and purpose for the talk of the body of Christ. I hope to lay a solid biblical foundation for understanding communication by starting where we first hear words spoken, then moving to the Fall to see the part words played in this world-altering event, and finally considering words from the vantage point of redemption. All the talk in the world is related to these events. Understanding this will orient us to the significance of our words, the reasons we struggle so much with them, and the design God has for the talk of his people.

Most communication books focus on techniques and skills without any recognition that our struggle with words goes much deeper. The war of words has its roots in the Garden of Eden. As you understand how these moments shaped our world of talk, you will begin to understand your own struggle with words and the way out that God has provided. This book will take an honest look at the problem so that it can offer you change that is more than temporary and cosmetic. If you understand the roots of your trouble, you can experience change that will last.

God Speaks!

You do not really understand the significance of words until you realize that the first words that human ears ever heard were not the words of another human being, but the words of God! The value of every piece of human communication is rooted in the fact that *God* speaks. Into the sights and sounds of the newly created world came the voice of God, speaking words of human language to Adam and Eve. When God chose to reveal himself that way, he raised talk to a place of highest significance as his primary vehicle of truth. Through words, we would come to know the most important truths that could be known—truths that reveal God's existence and glory, truths that give life. As we seek to understand the world of human talk, it is vital that we understand it from the perspective of Genesis 1—the only time in human history when there was no war of words.

In Genesis 1, the world of communication was a world of peace, truth, and life. Words were never used as weapons. Truth was never used to tear down. Words were always spoken in love, and human communication never broke the bonds of peace.

It is a world that can teach us a lot about communication. First, *God reveals himself, his plan, and his purpose in words.* Immediately after creating Adam and Eve, God spoke to them. It was his choice to reveal himself, to define his will, and to give identity to Adam and Eve by means of human language. All of his other means of self-revelation were explained and defined by this one central means.

God, the sovereign Creator and Lord, spoke to Adam and Eve in words that they could understand! Let the wonder of this grip you. The infinite and almighty One makes himself knowable and understandable through human language! From the moment of creation, God is not distant and aloof. He is not hiding in silence. He comes near and uses words to reveal himself and explain everything else. God is not just a God who *does*, he is a God who *speaks*—powerfully, elaborately, consistently, comprehensively, and clearly to his people. Each phase of his work is marked by his words. He does not leave his people without a witness.

God's communication is lovingly designed to address the need of the moment in simple words that can be understood. Before he works, God reveals what he is about to do; as he is working, he talks of what he is doing; and when he has finished, he interprets what he has done. He is a God who can be known because he is a God who speaks. Scripture presents him as the great standard for all communication.

Through his words God defines his character, his will, his plan and purpose, and his truth. Words like *rock, sun, fortress, shield, shepherd, father, judge, lamb, door, master, water,* and *bread* explain who he is and what he is doing. We are so familiar with these words that we tend to forget their significance. But these are the words by which we have come to know the King of Kings and the Lord of Lords! You cannot understand human communication without starting here, with the glory of God and his amazing grace in revealing himself to us in terms we understand, yet which radically alter our perspective on all that is.

No better example exists than the words of Isaiah 40.

> *You who bring good tidings to Zion,*
> *go up on a high mountain.*
> *You who bring good tidings to Jerusalem,*
> *lift up your voice with a shout,*
> *lift it up, do not be afraid;*

say to the towns of Judah,
   "Here is your God!"
See, the Sovereign LORD comes with power,
   and his arm rules for him.
See, his reward is with him,
   and his recompense accompanies him.
He tends his flock like a shepherd:
   He gathers the lambs in his arms
and carries them close to his heart;
   he gently leads those that have young.

Who has measured the waters in the hollow of his hand,
   or with the breadth of his hand marked off the heavens?
Who has held the dust of the earth in a basket,
   or weighed the mountains on the scales
   and the hills in a balance?
Who has understood the mind of the LORD,
   or instructed him as his counselor?
Whom did the LORD consult to enlighten him,
   and who taught him the right way?
Who was it that taught him knowledge
   or showed him the path of understanding?

Surely the nations are like a drop in a bucket;
   they are regarded as dust on the scales;
   he weighs the islands as though they were fine dust.
Lebanon is not sufficient for altar fires,
   nor its animals enough for burnt offerings.
Before him all the nations are as nothing;
   they are regarded by him as worthless
   and less than nothing.

To whom, then, will you compare God?
   What image will you compare him to?
As for an idol, a craftsman casts it,
   and a goldsmith overlays it with gold

and fashions silver chains for it.
A man too poor to present such an offering
selects wood that will not rot.
He looks for a skilled craftsman
to set up an idol that will not topple.

Do you not know?
Have you not heard?
Has it not been told you from the beginning?
Have you not understood since the earth was founded?
He sits enthroned above the circle of the earth,
and its peoples are like grasshoppers.
He stretches out the heavens like a canopy,
and spreads them out like a tent to live in.
He brings princes to naught
and reduces the rulers of this world to nothing.
No sooner are they planted,
no sooner are they sown,
no sooner do they take root in the ground,
than he blows on them and they wither,
and a whirlwind sweeps them away like chaff.

"To whom will you compare me?
Or who is my equal?" says the Holy One.
Lift up your eyes and look to the heavens:
Who created all these?
He who brings out the starry host one by one,
and calls them each by name.
Because of his great power and mighty strength,
not one of them is missing.

Why do you say, O Jacob,
and complain, O Israel,
"My way is hidden from the LORD;
my cause is disregarded by my God"?
Do you not know?

Have you not heard?
The LORD is the everlasting God,
the Creator of the ends of the earth.
He will not grow tired or weary,
and his understanding no one can fathom.
He gives strength to the weary
and increases the power of the weak.
Even youths grow tired and weary,
and young men stumble and fall;
but those who hope in the LORD
will renew their strength.
They will soar on wings like eagles;
they will run and not grow weary,
they will walk and not be faint. (vv. 9–31)

Here is human language at its highest, functioning as the window through which God is seen.

God's words not only define him, they define his creation as well. They give identity, meaning, and purpose to all God has created. We only know *ourselves* when we listen to the words he has spoken about us. God tells us who we are, defines what we are to do and the way we are to do it. None of these things could we discover on our own! The only hope for Adam and Eve was that God would speak to them, giving them identity and purpose, and making sense out of the world in which they had been placed.

God's words set boundaries and give freedom. His words create life and bring death. God created talk and his first words to Adam and Eve demonstrate its significance. Words are not cheap. Words reveal, define, explain, and shape.

People Speak

As we look at communication from the vantage point of creation, we also need to notice that *Adam and Eve talk.* Perhaps this point seems too obvious to bear mentioning, but we should not let its significance slip by us. Adam and Eve's ability to communicate in words made them unique in all of creation. They could take their thoughts, desires, and emotions and share them with each other. They were like God; they could talk! By giving them this ability, God was setting the shape of their lives.

There is nothing we depend on more than our ability to give and receive communication. In quiet conversation over coffee, in anxious conversation in a busy airport, in defending why we are late for a curfew or didn't complete the task at work, we talk. In teaching our children or intervening in an argument, in a lengthy congressional debate or an intense discussion with a friend, people talk. In a quiet good night, in words of athletic challenge, in romantic words of love, in words of correction and rebuke, anger and irritation, people talk. In the confusing patter on a railway platform in India, with the voices of children walking home from school in Soweto, people talk.

Words direct our existence and our relationships. They shape our observations and define our experiences. We really come to know other people through conversation. We want to be alone when we have heard too many words and we feel alone when it has been a while since anyone has spoken to us.

In creating us with the ability to talk, God has not only set us apart from the rest of creation, but he has determined the nature of our lives and relationships. Want to learn? Listen and talk. Want to have a relationship? Listen and talk. Want to get a job? Listen and talk. Want to worship? Listen and talk. Want to parent your children? Listen and talk. Want to contribute to the body of Christ? Listen and talk. People communicate; it is the nature of our existence. Words affect all the other things we do as human beings. God created our talk and gave it its value.

In Genesis 1 there was a simplicity and beauty to the world of human communication. There was no communication struggle, no war of words. Everything that was spoken reflected the glory of God. There were no arguments and lies, no words of hate, no impatient, irritated retorts. There was no yelling, cursing, or condemnation. There were no words spoken in pride, no deceptive, manipulative words, and no selfish ones. There were only true words, kindly and lovingly spoken, and thus no need for a book like this on communication. Every word met the standard of God's example and design.

Sadly, the world of Genesis 1 is long gone. The wonderful gift of communication has become the source of much sin and suffering. Too often, human beings speak and ignore God's design, destroying what he has made. As we look back with wonder at Genesis 1, we need to look forward to the day when the war of words will be over, when we will be with God and be like him, speaking only as he has designed, forever.

Words Interpret

There is one more thing we can learn from Genesis 1 about words. *Words define, explain, and interpret.* Even though Adam and Eve were perfect people living in a perfect world in a perfect relationship with God, they still needed God to talk to them. Their world needed definition. They needed to understand themselves and to understand life. Everything needed to be interpreted, and for this Adam and Eve were dependent on God. They could not figure things out on their own. Whatever discoveries they would make about the world and their lives would need to be explained and defined by the words of God. Words interpret. Human communication, like God's, is all about organizing, interpreting, and explaining the world around us.

From the silly little explanations that come from the mouths of children ("Mommy, I know how balloons work") to the searching questions of teenagers ("Why is it so important to be celibate before marriage?") to the frustrated questions of the adult ("Why does it seem as if I work constantly, yet there is never enough money to go around?"), people use words to communicate the meaning they have assigned to things.

Little children exhaust their parents with a thousand "whys" a week because they want to understand their world. Teenagers spend endless hours on the phone discussing the events of the day with their friends. The old man sits in the park with his friend looking back at life, wondering aloud what it was all about. We talk because we want to know; in order to know, we must talk. Talk is not cheap because interpretation is not cheap. The way we interpret life determines how we will respond to it.

Genesis 1 and Our Talk

What should we take away from our consideration of communication in Genesis 1? First, our words belong to the Lord. He is the Great Speaker. The wonder, the significance, the glory of human communication has its roots in *his* glory and in his decision to talk with us and allow us to talk with him and others. God has unlocked the doors of truth to us, using words as his key. The only reason we understand anything is that he has spoken. Words belong to God, but he has lent them to us so that we might know him and be used by him.

This means that words do not belong to us. Every word we speak must be up to God's standard and according to his design. They should echo the Great Speaker and reflect his glory. When we lose sight of this, our words lose their only shelter from difficulty. Talk was created by God for *his* purpose. Our words belong to him.

Getting Personal: Communication Self-Evaluation

Below are some of the fruits of godly talk (see Gal. 5:22–23). Evaluate yourself as you begin this book.

1. Does your talk with others lead to biblical problem solving?
2. Does your talk have a "stand together" or a "me against him/her/them" posture?
3. Do your words encourage others to be open and honest about their thoughts and feelings?
4. Are you approachable and teachable or defensive and self-protective when talking with others?
5. Is your communication healthy in the principal relationships in your life?
   - parent-child
   - husband-wife
   - extended family
   - sibling relationships
   - employer-employee
   - friend-friend
   - body of Christ
   - neighbor-neighbor
6. Does your talk encourage faith and personal spiritual growth in those around you?
7. Do you talk with others to develop relationships with them, or do you only talk to solve problems during times of trouble?
8. Do you speak humble and honest words of confession when you sin and words of sincere forgiveness when others sin against you?
9. Do your words reflect a willingness to serve others or a demand that they serve you?
10. As you face the struggles of talk, do you do so with a recognition of the gospel—God's forgiveness, his enabling grace, and the sanctifying work of the Holy Spirit?

I encourage you to start your reading of this book with honest self-examination. Confess your sins to God and others, and commit yourself to the work of change as you continue to read.

Chapter Two

Satan Speaks

Now the
serpent . . . said
to the woman . . .
(Gen. 3:1)

IT started out as a great day. The weather was as wonderful as we had hoped it would be, and we had just had a nice family breakfast together. I was looking forward to the day. We were going to leave for the activity we had planned in about two hours, so I was using the time to do some reading. But my teenaged daughter and my youngest son seemed to be more at each other's throats than usual. I was listening to the verbal back-and-forth escalate, growing more irritated with each moment. I sat there steaming with the book in my hand, but I refused to intervene. *I don't have to deal with this today,* I reasoned. *This is my day off.* I even wondered why my wife didn't do something. Didn't *she* hear what was going on?

Then my son ran into the bathroom with my daughter chasing him. They began to push with all their might on either side of the door, and I came to the end of my rope. I got up, not with a godly sense of parental purpose, but with a heart full of anger and self-pity. Didn't they know what my life is like? Didn't they know how hard I worked for them? Didn't they realize how important this day was to me? Couldn't they see I was trying to read? Couldn't they figure out that this was the kind of stuff that wrecks days like this? My daughter was the older, so why didn't she put a stop to it? Why did she have to be so stubborn?

In that spirit I got up and marched toward the scene. I saw my daughter first. I spoke to her out of my sense that I had been personally wronged, that she was wrecking *my* day, and that she didn't seem to care. I gave her the "I do and do for you and this is the thanks I get, why don't you grow up for once?" speech. My words were accusatory and harsh, born more out of a love for myself than for her. They were not spoken to accomplish what God wanted in that moment, but what I wanted. My daughter kept saying (as I talked on and on), "But Dad, you just don't understand." But I wasn't there to understand. I was there to vent my irritation.

I left her room and threw myself angrily down on the couch to resume reading, but I could not concentrate. My conscience was troubled over the way I had handled things. No matter how hard I tried to justify myself, I could not lift the weight of conviction, which soon turned to remorse. *When would I ever get it right? How could I know what I know and yet give in to this kind of communication?* I cried out in prayer for forgiveness and help. It was, for me, one of those "O, wretched man that I am" moments. I finished praying and went to my daughter's room to ask for her forgiveness.

Paradise Lost

If we are at all honest, we know that we do not live in the wonderful world of Genesis 1 any longer, where every word spoken was consistent with God's standard and design. This is no doubt why you are reading this book. It is certainly what prompted me to write it. In the Garden of Eden, there were no sins of talk. What happened? Why has simple human communication become such an occasion of sin and struggle? Why is it so hard for us to speak as God designed?

As we try to develop a biblical understanding of communication, unfortunately we cannot stop at Genesis 1. While it is still true that God speaks and that everything *we* say is rooted in his words to us, there was another speaker in the Garden. His arrival began the great war of words we now fight daily.

Now the serpent was more crafty than any of the wild animals the LORD God had made. He said to the woman, "Did God really say, 'You must not eat from any tree in the garden'?"

The woman said to the serpent, "We may eat fruit from the trees in the garden, but God did say, 'You must not eat fruit from the tree that is in the middle of the garden, and you must not touch it, or you will die.'"

"You will not surely die," the serpent said to the woman. "For God knows that when you eat of it your eyes will be opened, and you will be like God, knowing good and evil."

When the woman saw that the fruit of the tree was good for food and pleasing to the eye, and also desirable for gaining wisdom, she took some and ate it. She also gave some to her husband, who was with her, and he ate it. Then the eyes of both of them were opened, and they realized they were naked; so they sewed fig leaves together and made coverings for themselves.

Then the man and his wife heard the sound of the LORD God as he was walking in the garden in the cool of the day, and they hid from the LORD God among the trees of the garden. But the LORD God called to the man, "Where are you?"

He answered, "I heard you in the garden, and I was afraid because I was naked; so I hid."

And he said, "Who told you that you were naked? Have you eaten from the tree that I commanded you not to eat from?"

The man said, "The woman you put here with me—she gave me some fruit from the tree, and I ate it."

Then the LORD God said to the woman, "What is this you have done?"

The woman said, "The serpent deceived me, and I ate."
(Gen. 3:1–13)

Into the perfect world of the Garden came the voice of the Serpent. For the first time, the position, the authority, and the very words of God were being challenged. For the first time, words were spoken that were not consistent with God's standard and design. Satan spoke, and with his words the simple world of human communication became a confusing arena of sin and struggle. All of our trouble with talk has its roots here, in this dramatic moment of change in the Garden. In the world of communication, there are many trouble-generating "firsts" here.

Dramatic Change, Lasting Trouble

For the first time *the authority of God is challenged.* Until this moment, there were no verbal challenges to God's authority on earth. The world God had made existed in complete submission to his authority and will. Adam and Eve were obediently living out their identity as God's creatures, his image-bearers, and his resident managers on earth. All of their responses to God and their conversations with each other were carried out with unbroken submission to God. What took place in the moment the Serpent spoke is dramatic and unthinkable. Words were spoken that challenged God's authority! The world would never be the same again.

Imagine what our lives would be like if all of our words were spoken out of perfect submission to God. How much less complicated our lives would be! Many of the problems we experience when talking with one another emerge from the fact that we have usurped the authority of God: We say what we want to say, when and how we want to say it. We speak as if we are in charge and as if we have the right to use words to advance *our* purpose, and to achieve what would make *us* happy. We speak as if we were God rather than his creatures, called to submit to his authority in every idle word we speak. The problem with the way I spoke to my daughter was that I entered the room as if I were God, rather than a man under God's authority, with a heartfelt desire to see his will done in my life *and* my daughter's.

Many Voices, Many Interpretations

In that moment in the Garden we also see an *interpretation of life different from God's* for the first time. Recognize what Satan is doing here. He is taking the same set of facts that God interpreted for Adam and Eve and giving them a radically different spin. If his interpretation was believed, the listener would no longer think it was good, right, or necessary to obey God. In fact, one could say that if the Serpent's interpretation were right, it would be *stupid* to continue to obey God. Never before on earth had there been an interpretation opposing God's. Everything Adam and Eve understood about their world had been based on the interpretation God had given them.

Today we live in a confusing world of many interpretations. Most of them do not recognize the authority of God or operate with any desire to view life in a way that is consistent with his Word. This raises an extremely important point: you and I do not respond to the people or circumstances of our lives on the basis of the *facts*. Our responses are based on the way we *interpret* those facts. When I went to speak to my daughter, I was not responding simply to what had happened, but to the interpretation I had made about it. My interpretation, unfortunately, was selfish and self-righteous. I looked at my children's misbehavior only from the vantage point of all that *I* wanted and all that *I* had done. I did not even consider God's perspective on the situation. When I did, I was filled with conviction and remorse.

Many of our problems with words would be solved if we simply paused and asked ourselves how God would evaluate and respond to the present situation. We just let our thoughts run without challenging them. But if our interpretation of events is wrong, our words will not be right.

This is a principle that we do not want to miss: *Word problems are often interpretation problems.* We do not say the right thing because we do not believe the right thing. This is what happened in the Garden. A Pandora's box of trouble opened as, for the first time, Adam and Eve heard and believed an interpretation that was not consistent with God's. Satan's voice was the first of thousands of voices that would come to challenge what God has spoken.

When an enraged father stands over his teenaged son and says, "I don't care what it takes—if it is the last thing I do, I'll get you to respect me!" he has spoken words that stand in opposition to God's words to him as a father. When a wife says to her husband, "In all my other relationships I am okay, but you make me so angry," her words reflect an interpretation of her own anger that stands in opposition to what God says. When a worker says, "If he hadn't given the job to her, I wouldn't be so bitter," his problem is not just his words, but the attitudes behind them. In each example, what is wrong is not just vocabulary and tone of voice, but a way of looking at life that does not agree with what God says is right and true. As we see in Genesis 3, word problems are often interpretation problems.

Listening to Lies

When the Serpent speaks in the Garden, there is another problem. For the first time, *a lie is spoken.* Until that moment, every conversation was perfectly, completely truthful. God's words were utterly reliable, and life could be built upon them. Adam and Eve's words to each other were trustworthy because they were consistent with the words of God. But here, shockingly, the Serpent purposely lies to advance his purpose. He is not mistaken; he has not forgotten what is true. He is not ignorant or lacking in understanding. He *knows* that what he is saying is untrue. That is *why* he says it! He does not want Adam and Eve to live in the light of truth or in obedience to God. He seeks to sell them a lie and he seeks to make that lie plausible.

It is, again, a moment of dramatic change. Good, godly communication is always dependent on truth. Lies, falsehood, and deception always subvert it. Lies not only distort facts, but they destroy the trust necessary for people to talk with one another. Every word we speak is rooted either in the truth or in a lie. Most of our communication problems come because we deceive, distort, and manipulate with our words. We reshape the facts to our advantage. We recast events, often to the point of convincing ourselves that our perspective is true. When I walked into my daughter's room that morning, I was fully convinced that I was right in what I was about to do. But I had bought into a lie.

Accusations and Blame

The Serpent's words brought about another first that day in the Garden: for the first time, *people spoke against one another.* Up to this point there had been no critical, condemning, angry words. There had been no accusations or put-downs, no throwing a person's words or actions back in his or her face. Adam and Eve's relationship was free of this for they were yet free of sin. But after they ate the fruit, we see a dramatic change not only in their relationship with God, but in their relationship with each other. When God asks Adam about eating the forbidden fruit, Adam is quick to accuse Eve. He does not stand with her, he does not protect her. He does not act as an intercessor and advocate, pleading her case to God. Rather, he stands aside, points a finger, and essentially says, "Blame her, God, she's the one who got me into this mess."

How much of our communication is about passing the blame to others! "You make me so angry!" "If you hadn't _____, then I wouldn't have _____." "I was never this way before I met you!" "Whenever you do that, I just can't control myself." "I was never this uptight before I had children." "If you weren't such a good cook, I wouldn't have this weight problem."

Who among us isn't tempted to accuse and blame when the heat of responsibility is put on us? In times of difficulty, we often are more ready to assess blame than to seek solutions. Barely a day goes by without blame being on our lips or in our ears.

But there is another dimension to this problem. For the first time, *words of accusation are spoken against God.* When Adam is approached by God after he has eaten the fruit, he points the finger not only at Eve but *at God.* Adam says, "God, if you hadn't given me this woman, none of this would have happened. God, it's your fault; you created her and look what she has done to me now!" Just like Adam, when we blame people and situations for our problems, below the surface we are also making accusations against God.

When a husband says, "My wife makes me so angry!," his finger is pointed not only at his wife but at God, who ordained the relationship. A person who says, "I would be more active in the ministries of my church if I didn't have to work so hard to make ends meet," is essentially saying, "God, it is your fault. If you would do a better job of providing for me, I could serve you in the way I really desire." A parent who says, "I was much more relaxed and patient before I had children," is actually blaming God for the parental burden that he finds overwhelming. At the Fall, the God who is to be loved, obeyed, and served became the scapegoat for the sins of his people. In much of our talk today we hear the same subtle accusations against God.

Words that challenge God's authority, lies, false interpretations of life, accusations and blame against God and man all have their origin in this dramatic moment of change. Satan speaks, and as Adam and Eve act upon his words, the world of talk becomes a world of trouble. No longer do we simply reflect the image of God with our words; we also reflect the image of the Serpent. No longer do we consistently speak up to God's standard; we often speak down to the Serpent's. No longer are our words a faithful picture of God's design; too often they picture Satan's deceit. Talk is no longer easy or safe. Instead, we live in a world where lies manipulate, angry words wound, falsehood destroys, slander harms, condemnation tears down, and disrespectful words challenge the authorities God has set in place.

Who among us has not regretted things we have said as a parent, a spouse, a friend, a neighbor, or a worker? Which of us has not longed to snatch back our words—to somehow erase the tape—so that they would no longer exist in memory? Who among us has not had to go back repeatedly to our children, our spouses, or our friends to ask forgiveness for the things we said or for the way we said them?

A Restless Evil

James captures this world of trouble with dramatic words. He alerts us to the amount and significance of the damage that can be done through our words.

> *When we put bits into the mouths of horses to make them obey us, we can turn the whole animal. Or take ships as an example. Although they are so large and are driven by strong winds, they are steered by a very small rudder wherever the pilot wants to go. Likewise the tongue is a small part of the*

body, but it makes great boasts. Consider what a great forest is set on fire by a small spark. The tongue also is a fire, a world of evil among the parts of the body. It corrupts the whole person, sets the whole course of his life on fire, and is itself set on fire by hell.

All kinds of animals, birds, reptiles, and creatures of the sea are being tamed and have been tamed by man, but no man can tame the tongue. It is a restless evil, full of deadly poison.

With the tongue we praise our Lord and Father, and with it we curse men, who have been made in God's likeness. Out of the same mouth come praise and cursing. My brothers, this should not be. Can both fresh water and salt water flow from the same spring? My brothers, can a fig tree bear olives, or a grapevine bear figs? Neither can a salt spring produce fresh water. (James 3:3–12)

For James, the tongue is a "world of evil," "corrupting the whole person," and "setting the whole course of his life on fire." He says it is like a bit, a rudder, a spark, and an untameable animal. With our talk, either we are imaging our Creator and Lord, or we are imaging the Serpent, Satan. Our words build and give life or they tear down and destroy. They are important.

The War of Words

Proverbs also depicts the war of words that is so much a part of life in the fallen world. Here are some representative passages:

Wisdom will save you from the ways of wicked men,
   from men whose words are perverse. (2:12)

It will save you also from the adulteress,
   from the wayward wife with her seductive words. (2:16)

If you have been trapped by what you said,
    ensnared by the words of your mouth,
then do this, my son, to free yourself,
    since you have fallen into your neighbor's hands:
Go and humble yourself;
    press your plea with your neighbor! (6:2–3)

There are six things the LORD hates,
    seven that are detestable to him:
        haughty eyes,
        a lying tongue,
        hands that shed innocent blood,
        a heart that devises wicked schemes,
        feet that are quick to rush into evil,
        a false witness who pours out lies
        and a man who stirs up dissension among brothers.
    (6:16–19)

With persuasive words she led him astray;
    she seduced him with her smooth talk. (7:21)

When words are many, sin is not absent,
    but he who holds his tongue is wise. (10:19)

The words of the wicked lie in wait for blood,
    but the speech of the upright rescues them. (12:6)

A truthful witness gives honest testimony,
    but a false witness tells lies.
Reckless words pierce like a sword,
    but the tongue of the wise brings healing.
Truthful lips endure forever,
    but a lying tongue lasts only a moment. (12:17–19)

A scoundrel plots evil,
    and his speech is like a scorching fire.

A perverse man stirs up dissension,
*   and a gossip separates close friends. (16:28)*

A wicked man listens to evil lips;
*   a liar pays attention to a malicious tongue. (17:4)*

Arrogant lips are unsuited to a fool—
*   how much worse lying lips to a ruler! (17:7)*

Starting a quarrel is like breaching a dam;
*   so drop the matter before a dispute breaks out. (17:14)*

He who loves a quarrel loves sin;
*   he who builds a high gate invites destruction. (17:19)*

A fool finds no pleasure in understanding
*   but delights in airing his own opinions. (18:2)*

The words of a gossip are like choice morsels;
*   they go down to a man's inmost parts. (18:8)*

The tongue has the power of life and death,
*   and those who love it will eat its fruit. (18:21)*

A corrupt witness mocks at justice,
*   and the mouth of the wicked gulps down evil.*
Penalties are prepared for mockers,
*   and beatings for the backs of fools. (19:28–29)*

Better to live on a corner of the roof
*   than share a house with a quarrelsome wife. (21:9)*

Drive out the mocker, and out goes strife;
*   quarrels and insults are ended. (22:10)*

If you argue your case with a neighbor,
*   do not betray another man's confidence,*

or he who hears it may shame you
and you will never lose your bad reputation. (25:9–10)

Without wood a fire goes out;
without gossip a quarrel dies down.
As charcoal to embers and as wood to fire,
so is a quarrelsome man for kindling strife. (26:20–21)

A quarrelsome wife is like
a constant dripping on a rainy day;
restraining her is like restraining the wind
or grasping oil with the hand. (27:15–16)

He who rebukes a man will in the end gain more favor
than he who has a flattering tongue. (28:23)

Whoever flatters his neighbor
is spreading a net for his feet. (29:5)

Mockers stir up a city,
but wise men turn away anger. (29:8)

Do you see a man who speaks in haste?
There is more hope for a fool than for him. (29:20)

This is just a representative list of passages, yet the Proverbs pointedly depict the "world of evil" that is the tongue. This world is pictured in every book of Scripture. We need to humbly confess that there *is* trouble with our talk. The words of James and the Proverbs depict us. We have not spoken in a way that upholds God's standard and design. We often have descended to the standard of the Father of Lies, the one who deceives, divides, and destroys—Satan himself.

We have laid traps with our mouths. We have seduced with our words. Our talk has stirred up dissension. We have said too much and spoken in haste. Our words have been reckless.

We have given in to gossip and in our anger our words have been malicious. We have been quarrelsome. At times, we have delighted to air our own opinions. We have given in to mocking humor. We have betrayed the confidence of others with our words.

Genesis 3 and Our Words

What should we take away from our consideration of communication in Genesis 3? We must begin by humbly acknowledging that our words have their roots not only in the words of the Lord (Gen. 1), but also in the words of the Serpent (Gen. 3). With this admission we confess that our communication struggle is not primarily a struggle of technique, but a struggle of the heart. Our war of words is not with other people; it is a battle within. Will we speak in a way that images the Lord, the Great Speaker, or the Serpent, the Great Deceiver? Who will control our hearts and our words?

The war of words introduced in Genesis 1 and 3 is depicted throughout the rest of Scripture. We fight it daily in our own lives. Our words now divide, deceive, and destroy. They are a world of evil, causing a world of trouble. Talk is not cheap. Its cost is great.

How do we deal with this problem? Each of us needs to say, "Lord, these passages expose me. I admit that I have not always recognized that my words belong to you. I have not faithfully communicated according to your example and plan. I have claimed my words as my own, to be used for my own purpose. I have listened to the Great Deceiver and at many times and in many ways spoken more like him than you. I ask for your forgiveness and I plead for your help. I know that you alone are able to tame my tongue. I offer my talk back to you, that I may speak up to your standard and according to your design."

And as we confess, we need to embrace the glorious

promise of the gospel captured by Paul in 2 Corinthians 12:9: "My grace is sufficient for you, for my power is made perfect in weakness." Nowhere is our weakness more dramatically revealed than in our struggle with words. But we need not despair. Christ has come. He has lived, died, and risen for us! In him we find not only forgiveness, but deliverance from sins of the heart that lead to sins of the tongue. In utter weakness, our hearts can be filled with joy as we reflect on the grandeur of Christ's provision. In him our words find their hope.

Getting Personal:
A Time for Confession

Evaluate your world of talk. Are there places where your words have followed the pattern of the enemy more than the Lord? Take time to consider, pray, and confess. Confess to God and the people with whom you live and work.

1. Are there places where your words challenge the authority of God? (Seeking to take wrongful control, speaking words of condemnation, punishing others with words, undermining the authority of God-appointed leaders, grumbling and complaining about the situations God has ordained for your life, etc.)

2. Do your words reveal places where you have bought into an interpretation of life different from the Lord's (as revealed in Scripture)? In other words, does your talk reveal a consistent, biblical view of life that encourages others to look at life the same way? (Example: Outbursts of anger during a traffic jam versus using the time to have a wholesome conversation with your wife and children.)

3. Has your communication been infected with Satan's lie that the things you need for life can be found outside of Christ? Examples:

- "I must win this argument."
- "I must have her love, appreciation, and respect."
- "I will get him to admit _____ if it's the last thing I do!"
- "This is *the* way it *has* to be done."
- "I cannot live with _____."
- "I have the right to my happiness."

Remember, Christ not only forgives, he delivers. He not only delivers, he restores. He not only restores, he reconciles.

Chapter Three

The Word in the Flesh

The Word became flesh and blood and moved into the neighborhood. (John 1:14)

I have been married for over a quarter of a century. God has given me a godly wife who has more character than I do. Luella and I enjoy a wonderful relationship in many ways. We were both raised in Christian homes where we were taught the truth from infancy. Both of us came to Christ as children and were educated at a Christian college. We have spent our lives in ministry and have been blessed to sit under fine biblical teaching. We have worked hard to follow Christ's design for our marriage.

We spend time together weekly outside the home to talk about issues that need to be discussed. We have tried through the years to have daily family worship. Yet as I was preparing this book, I recognized that despite all of this, we are not free of trouble in our communication. I don't mean that we are screaming and yelling. We are not always angry and at each other's throats. But we don't have to look back very far to see sin in our talk. It may have been a word hastily and thoughtlessly spoken, a word of irritation, a quick accusation, a selfish comment or demand, an "I told you so" where a word of comfort or encouragement was needed. It might have been an impatient retort, a moment of needless nit-picking, a comment filled with self-righteousness or self-pity, or a situation where past sins are resurrected for a moment.

Even with all of the scriptural teaching we have received, with all of our personal commitment and practical effort, with all of our pleas for forgiveness and prayers for help, as a couple we still have problems with our talk. This is how great our need is! This is how deep our problem is!

Our Tendency to Forget

When I go to Christian bookstores, I sometimes wonder if we have forgotten what our real problem is. Do we really think that we are going to solve life-long communication problems with human insights and snazzy techniques? Have we forgotten that communication problems reveal problems at a much deeper and more fundamental level? If we do not tackle these deeper issues, we will never solve the problems of our daily communication. If knowledge and skill were all we needed, Luella and I would have solved the problems with our talk long ago. But we need something deeper than technique, skill, and knowledge. Every day this deep need is revealed as our family communicates.

Recently I watched my sons argue with each other. This was nothing new; they are two years apart and have had many arguments. In fact, this particular argument is one they have had many times before. Yet this time it captured my attention. Their words were laden with accusation. Their tone was angry. No one stopped to listen as the volley of words escalated and the volume increased. It wasn't long before they had abandoned the issue at hand to hurl hurts from the past at each other. They both spoke out of pain, frustration and anger, impatience and jealousy. They weren't speaking to solve problems or listening to understand. Their words were simply weapons in a war. Each of them wanted to silence the other and *win*. Their sentences were full of "you always" and "you never." They both stood there, wrapped in their robes of self-righteousness, feeling quite justified in accusing the other. And even though they kept on ventilating, they both communicated the belief that they were wasting their time. They were sure that the other would never "get it."

As I listened, two thoughts gripped me. The first was that I didn't want to have to deal with this "war" the first thing in the morning. But the second thought was more theological and more gripping. I realized that I had never taught my boys how to argue and fight. I had never taught them how to wound each other with words. I had never lectured them on the right moment to dump a record of wrongs on another person. I had never sought to impart to them the skills of accusation and condemnation. Yet my sons fenced with confidence and skill. They had a natural talent to use words to do exactly what their angry hearts desired.

As I began to intervene, my heart was filled with sadness. I could stop the argument, but I could not change what really needed to be changed. Moreover, I was powerfully aware that what needed to be changed within them still needed to be changed within me. In our home there is seldom a few hours (let alone a whole day) that goes by without some kind of conflict! (And, believe it or not, we have a family that is doing pretty well.) How deep is our need! I spoke to my boys with tears that morning, because for once I was more gripped by the gravity of our spiritual need than by my frustration over another petty quarrel to solve.

Perhaps you are wondering if my boys would benefit from learning better communication techniques or a better sense of location and timing. No doubt they would, but the war of words that morning went much deeper than that. Deep spiritual needs were revealed that would not be alleviated by a few principles on good communication.

The Coming of the Word

How does God, the Great Speaker, address our need in this area? He does *not* demand that we meet his standard in our own strength. No, he sends his Son, the Word, to take on flesh, to live as a man and to be the most glorious of all of God's messages to us! *The Word became flesh.* Listen to the words of John.

> *In the beginning was the Word, and the Word was with God, and the Word was God. He was with God in the beginning.*
>
> *Through him all things were made; without him nothing was made that has been made. In him was life, and that life was the light of men. The light shines in the darkness, but the darkness has not understood it. . . .*
>
> *He was in the world, and though the world was made through him, the world did not recognize him. He came to that which was his own, but his own did not receive him. Yet to all who received him, to those who believed in his name, he gave the right to become children of God—children born not of natural descent, nor of human decision or a husband's will, but born of God.*
>
> *The Word became flesh and made his dwelling among us. We have seen his glory, the glory of the One and Only, who came from the Father, full of grace and truth.*
>
> *. . . From the fullness of his grace we have all received one blessing after another. For the law was given through Moses; grace and truth came through Jesus Christ. No one has ever seen God, but God the One and Only, who is at the Father's side, has made him known. (John 1:1–5, 10–14, 16–18)*

Think on this. The God who created speech and spoke the world into existence, the God who used human words to reveal himself to his people throughout the ages, comes to his world as the Word, to people who have forsaken him. He is not only a speaker of truth, he *is* Truth, and only in him is there any hope for us. Only in the Word do we find hope to win the war of words and speak again according to our Maker's example and design. The Word became flesh because there was no other way to fix what is broken in us.

The fact that the Word came in the flesh tells us something very significant about our trouble with talk: Our problem is not fundamentally one of ignorance or ineptness. Remember the words of James: "All kinds of animals, birds, reptiles and creatures of the sea are being tamed and have been tamed by man, but no man can tame the tongue. It is a restless evil, full of deadly poison" (James 3:7–8). James's point is that our communication problems cannot be solved by normal human means. Changes in location, situation, education, training, exercise, or the nature of the relationship will not solve the problem. The tongue is humanly untameable! It is a powerful, restless evil that leaves all of us confounded.

The War Beneath the War of Words

There is a fundamental biblical observation we need to make at this point: *The Word would not have come to our world if our struggle were primarily a struggle of flesh and blood.* The problem with our words is an intensely spiritual one, a problem of the human heart. Perhaps you're a wife who is very hurt by the way your husband communicates with you. Or maybe you're a teenager, and it's hard not to feel condemned by the way your parents talk to you. Maybe you're a husband who is bitter over the lack of respect given to you by your family. Each of us has been personally hurt by the words of others, and each of us has spoken words that have stung others. Because of this, it is important to recognize that the war of words is actually the fruit of a greater, more fundamental war. This war is the war of wars; it is what life is about. Paul refers to this war in Ephesians 6:12 when he says, "For our struggle is not against flesh and blood, but against the rulers, against the authorities, against the powers of this dark world and against the spiritual forces of evil in the heavenly realms."

In Ephesians 4 Paul says a great deal about the talk of the body of Christ. He calls us to be "completely humble and gentle," to "be patient, bearing with one another in love," to "make every effort to keep the unity of the Spirit through the bond of peace," to speak "the truth in love," to "put off falsehood and speak truthfully to [your] neighbor." He says, "'In your anger do not sin.' Do not let the sun go down while you are still angry." He urges us to "not let any unwholesome talk come out of your mouths, but only what is helpful for building others up." He calls us "to get rid of all bitterness, rage, and anger, brawling and slander, along with every form of malice," to "be kind and compassionate to one another," and to "[forgive] each other, just as in Christ God forgave [us]." In Ephesians 5 and 6 Paul applies these principles to the church, the home, and the outside world.

You cannot read what Paul has to say without being impressed with the depth and scope of the commands. Perhaps you're thinking as you read, *Paul, you've got to be kidding! Completely humble and gentle talk in* our *home? No way! Communication that is free of all anger and malice? That will be the day!* Yet this *is* what Paul calls us to. And these commands *are* intended to help us.

You say, "They don't help me—they just leave me discouraged!" But maybe that is the point. When you face God's high standard for our words and see how far short we all fall from it, you are driven to recognize two things that are the focus of this chapter. First, you and I are immediately faced with the fact that we have grave problems in our communication that are much more fundamental than skill, technique, and vocabulary. The second fact flows from the first: Since our need runs deeper than technique, we need more than a training course or a new set of skills. We need the rescue that only Jesus, the living Word and our Redeemer, can provide.

So, when our best efforts to win the war of words have failed, we encounter the greatest hope of all. But it is not in us or our potential. It is in the Word and his presence, power, and promises. Because Jesus has come to live, die, and be raised for us, there is hope that we can speak as God has designed.

Life Is War

In light of that, Paul's words in Ephesians 6:12 could not be more practical. When Paul writes about spiritual warfare at the end of this letter, he is not changing the subject; he is summarizing everything he has said before (including all he has said about communication). Paul is zealous for us to realize that *life is war,* not with other people, but with *spiritual forces of evil in the heavenly realms*! *This* is what is being played out in the home, the church, the workplace, and the community. This war is what makes each of these forums difficult. We are not fighting only to get along with one another. Far more importantly, we are fighting to withstand the Devil's schemes against us!

Life is war. A dramatic conflict is underway between the forces of the Great Speaker and the Great Deceiver. While God is seeking to root us deeper in his life, his peace, and his truth, Satan seeks to uproot us by deceitful scheming, plausible lies, and cruel trickery. Like all wars, this war is for control. It is a war for our hearts. And if this spiritual war were not going on, there would be no war of words.

This amplifies our understanding of the gospel, of why it was necessary for Jesus to come. Jesus, the living Word, came as Revelation and Redeemer so that we would have what we need to stand our ground in the midst of conflict. In ourselves we are no match for these "spiritual forces of evil in the heavenly realms." So Christ came, not only as the Word but as the Second Adam. The first Adam represented us all, and when he faced Satan, he believed his lies, succumbed to his trickery, and fell into sin. Christ had to come as the Second Adam, again as our representative, to face Satan. Thus, before his public ministry, Christ faced his foe. Three times he was tempted with the same old lies and trickery. Three times he defeated Satan, demonstrating his power over the forces of evil and accomplishing a great victory for us (see Matt. 4:1–11; 12:22–29; Rom. 5:12–21).

Through his work, Christ empowers and equips us for the battle so that when the evil day comes, we will be able to stand firm, letting nothing move us away from the life to which he has called us. This life includes speaking in a way that is worthy of the gospel. Jesus' victory gained for us the ability to live at peace with him and one another.

This gives us a completely different perspective on the fight about who gets the bathroom first or who ate the last of the family's favorite cereal. The problem of these moments goes beyond the surface issues of too many people, too few bathrooms, and too many empty boxes of cereal. We are what is wrong in each situation. We are the common element in all of our communication problems. And it is vitally important that we neither minimize our problem (by saying that these moments are not important) nor give in to cynicism (by saying that there is no real hope of change). These little moments do matter, for they are where we live everyday. Yet there is hope of substantial change because Jesus Christ, the Word, the Redeemer, has given us every resource we need to speak as we are meant to speak.

The Right Resources for the Struggle

What has the Word given us so that we can speak up to God's standard and according to his design? In a brief prayer in Ephesians (1:15–23), Paul uses four dynamic words to capture the resources that are ours because of Christ's redeeming work.

The first word is *hope*. In the Word we find hope for our words. This hope is not a dreamy wish or an unfounded expectation. No, biblical hope is nothing less than *a confident expectation of a guaranteed result*. In him we can win the war of words. We do not have to settle for bitter, angry, destructive, divisive communication. We can have high standards and set lofty goals, not because of who we are, but because of what he has done. So we refuse to settle for the status quo, to let the creeping cynicism of hopelessness cause us to give up in the face of struggle. No, we live and speak with faith and courage, believing that something better can be achieved because of what he has done.

As a wife, you cannot let yourself believe that your marital communication will never improve. In the Word there is hope. As a husband, you cannot give in to your anger and the words that it dictates. There is hope. As a friend, you cannot refuse to talk in your moment of hurt, believing it won't matter. There is hope. As a parent, you must believe that you can minister to your children even out of your own hurt and exhaustion, because the Word has come and, with him, hope. Reader, ask yourself, Does my communication flow out of my confidence in the resource-giving work of the Word?

What is our hope of speaking in a godly manner when a rebellious teenager is resisting us? What is our hope of speaking as God designed with a distant husband, a critical wife, a bitter Christian friend, or a contentious neighbor? Where will we find the strength to speak rightly to a hard, demanding, unthankful boss or self-centered, complaining children? What hope do we have for wholesome communication when we enter a difficult conversation already tired and discouraged? What will we do when we struggle with our own bitterness, when we are angry or struggling with wanting our own way? What will help us when we feel falsely accused, unappreciated, unnoticed, or taken for granted? What is our hope of speaking in a way that promotes the work of God rather than the desires of our sinful natures? Our only hope is the Word. His work on our behalf totally alters the way we can respond to the struggle of words.

You know how it works. Most of our daily communication isn't organized and scripted. We are constantly thrust into moments that were not part of our agenda for the day.

Let's say that my son came to me one Thursday night at 10:30 and said, "Dad, I've got a science project due tomorrow and there are a few things I need." Bear in mind, he has known about this assignment for weeks! Trying to keep my composure, I ask him what he needs. "Well, I need some poster board," he says tentatively. "That's not too bad," I think. "We can piece together the cardboard that is lying around the house." "Anything else?" I ask. He says, "Well, I sorta need some markers." I can feel my irritation level rising, but I reason we can probably pour water into some of the dried-up markers lying around to get through one more project. Again I ask, "Is there anything else?" And with a frightened mumble he says, "Twelve baby chickens." I cannot believe what I'm hearing! I feel my face flush red. "Sure, I'll just run down to the all-night chicken store and pick up a fresh dozen!"

In a flash the war breaks out—no, not between my son and me, but within my heart. I'm angry and frustrated. I'm tired of the minefield of unexpected difficulty. There is a powerful draw to deal with the situation by beating him with words. I want to tell him how stupid he is and that he is nuts if he thinks I am going to help him. I want to tell him that in my day I never procrastinated with projects. There is a lot I want to say, and in that moment, I'd better have a hope that enables me to stand against everything I instinctively want to do!

If the war rages in our hearts in these little, mundane moments, how much more will it be present in moments of marital anguish, parental disappointment, and disillusioning failure in the body of Christ! Many of these moments cannot be avoided, but you will face them in a radically different manner if you believe that because of the work of the Word, there is hope for us. The next three words Paul uses describe that hope.

Everything We Need

The second word Paul uses in Ephesians 1:15–23 to capture the present benefits of the work of the Word is *riches*. Paul says that there are "glorious riches in Christ." What is he talking about here? Peter captures it well when he says that "his divine power has given us everything we need for life and godliness" (2 Peter 1:3). Not a lot, not more than most, but *everything* we need. Consider the words here. The verb in the passage ("has given") is in the perfect tense, which indicates an action in the past that has continuing results into the future. It means that Christ has already placed in my storehouse everything that I need. "To do what?" you may ask. Peter says, "everything for life and *godliness*." I have been given not just everything I need for eternal life, but everything I need to live a godly life from the time I am saved until the time God takes me home to be with him!

Let the power of these words sink in. The Lord will never put you in a situation without giving you everything you need to do what he has called you to do.

Let's say that you are a wife, who is in a very difficult conversation with your husband. There are riches in your storehouse for this moment. Perhaps you are a worker struggling with a very critical boss. Everything you need to speak in a godly way has already been given. Parent, you are facing another day with a rebellious and disrespectful teenager. All the riches that you need to move beyond your own hurt and anger and to function as an instrument of the Lord have been given. The Word has come and in his hands are glorious riches. His supply is the only thing that will tame the human tongue!

The third item in Paul's resource list is *power*. Paul puts it this way: "his incomparably great power for us who believe" (Eph. 1:19). Because of the work of the Word, we have power to win the war that fuels our struggles with words. We *do not* struggle with communication simply because we lack the skills or vocabulary. Our problem is powerlessness. Our problem is inability. That's why James asks the rhetorical question, Who can tame the tongue? The best biblical answer to the question is, No one this side of the Word! But Christ *has* come, demonstrating his power in his ministry, exercising his power over evil on the cross, and blessing his people with power in the person of the indwelling Holy Spirit. Paul says that God, who can do much, much more than anything we could ever ask or imagine, *is at work* by his power *within* us (see Eph. 3:20).

Consider this for a moment. God hasn't issued us a series of grand and lofty directives and then sat back to see if we would obey them. No, he understands that our sin has rendered us powerless, and that we will not *know* what we need to know and cannot *do* what we need to do apart from him. So he has unzipped us and gotten inside us by his Spirit. His inconceivable power is *within* us! And it is not only within, it is *at work*! Paul says that we have been given power that can be compared only to the power by which Christ was raised from the dead.

This changes everything. The Word has made us his dwelling place so that we would have the power to speak as he has designed. In him the impossible becomes possible. The war becomes winnable. The tongue becomes tameable, no longer an instrument of evil, but a producer of good.

What makes this book different from other communication books is not the author's vast storehouse of wisdom and experience. It is one thing: the gospel. It radically changes the way we understand and wage the war of words that is so much a part of the human struggle.

The gospel prevents us from having a communication model of *independent strength* that assumes that our problems can be solved with the right insights and skills. The gospel forces us to face our inability. The gospel also prevents us from having a communication model of *weakness and inability* that would cause us to look at God's goals and say, "If only we were able!" In Christ we embrace both inability and ability. The Word comes to fill us with his power precisely because we are so weak. But in Christ, we who could not stand now stand able!

Apply this to your world of talk. Power has been given. It resides with you by the Spirit and reaches to the point of your deepest communication weakness. Wife, it is a denial of the gospel to look at your husband and say to yourself, "Why bother? He can't change." Husband, it is a denial of the gospel to be self-righteous and defensive when your wife tries to talk to you about sin in your talk. Parents, you deny the gospel when you allow your communication with your child to be ruled by unrestrained emotions and desires. Because the Word has come and has given us his power, we can step forward in courage, believing that we can gain new ground in our world of talk.

Because of the indwelling presence of the Spirit of God, there is hope that the tongue can do the good God has ordained. None of us can say that we are too weak ("If only I had more faith," or "If only I had a little more courage," or "If I could only think of the right things to say"). None of us can blame our personalities ("I'm just an extrovert," or "I'm just too shy," or "I'm sorry, I'm just not a morning person"). None of us can blame our past ("I was never given a good example of communication," or "I was always taught to fight back," or "My parents never really spent any time teaching us"). None of us can blame people around us ("If I just had children who were more compliant," or "If my husband were more loving and affectionate, then I would . . ." or "If my wife weren't always criticizing me," or "If my boss were a little more appreciative of what I do for him everyday"). None of us can blame our present situations ("If only I had more time," or "If my job weren't so demanding").

Yes, we are living with sinners, our schedules are busy, many of us were raised in negative environments, and we have all been given different personalities that help and hinder us in various ways. But this is the point: God has given us his Spirit, not in spite of, but *because* of these realities. The Holy Spirit was given so that we can do the will of God even though we are sinners in a fallen world; so that his life and strength would overwhelm all of the effects of our own sin and the sin of others against us; so that we can actually do the will of God! His power is not distant and dormant; it is *at work* within us! We can speak up to God's standard and according to his design because he lives within us with mighty, active power.

Personal Redemptive Rule

The final word that summarizes the resources we have been given in Christ is *rule*. Paul says that Christ is "*head* over everything for the church, which is his body" (Eph. 1:22–23). There is no situation we will ever encounter that is not ruled by Christ. Our lives are not out of control. Christ carefully administers them for our benefit and his glory.

This idea of Christ's headship and rule goes right to the place in our communication where we often get into the most trouble. Often our words reveal an attempt to control things for our own good. We are moved by a personal sense of what we want or what we think would be good, and so we speak in a way that guarantees we will get it. We defend, accuse, inflict guilt, manipulate, rationalize, argue, cajole, beg, plead, or threaten, all for the purpose of controlling a person or a situation.

Sometimes we do this out of fear. It really does feel as if our lives are spinning out of control. It does seem as if the people around us are standing in the way of what is best. It seems right to take control. If we don't, then what will happen? But fear-driven talk forgets one of the most precious promises of the gospel: that Christ right now, at this moment, is ruling all things for our particular benefit as his children. I may not always see his hand and I won't always recognize the good he is doing, but he is active and ruling all the same. Communication that attempts to find personal security by taking control forgets one of the sweetest provisions of the Word, God's control over all things for his children.

Another way to say this is that our words often reveal that we are not so much trusting in the Lord as we are trying to *be* him. We are attempting to do with our words what only he can do. When we do, we will fail, hurting ourselves and those around us.

For example, a parent must not be so afraid of what will happen to his child that he tries to do with words what only God can accomplish by his grace: "If it's the last thing I ever do, I will get you to respect me" (threat). "Think of all of our hard work, think of all of the money we have spent, think of all the time we have invested—is this the thanks we get?" (guilt). "Remember that car you asked for on your birthday? If you do _____, you never know—you might find yourself holding the keys" (manipulation). In each example the speaker is trying to turn the child's heart with some kind of verbal tool.

But verbal attempts at control don't always flow out of fear. They often flow from pride. As sinners we tend to be selfish. We tend to struggle with contentment and enter every situation loaded with our own desires.

When I get up in the morning, very often the first person I think about is me! I am already filled with my own desires, rehearsing in my mind what I would like the day to be like. When I sit in my office and the phone rings, I often think, *What now?* fearful that someone is going to interfere with my plans. When I am driving home from work at night, I often find myself dreaming about what the evening will be like, wondering what disasters others will have brought into the house that will destroy my dream. Our words often reveal how utterly self-focused we are and how intent we are on getting what we want from others.

"Can't I just have one night's peace!" the father screams at the child who has asked for his help on an all-night project. "I don't think you really love me!" says the wife to her husband as he is rushing out the door, already late and now angry and frustrated as well. Her words are self-focused, ill-timed, and indifferent to the needs of her husband. "If I didn't live here, half of my problems would be gone!" moans the teenager who has been confronted with his poor attitude. Driven by what he wants, he is striking back at parents who always seem to be in the way.

The gospel speaks to this struggle as well. Christ calls us to an agenda higher than our own pleasure. Christ rules everything for us, but his rule has not been established so that we would be happy. We are called to submit ourselves to Christ so that we would be holy and so that our holiness would bring him glory.

The Word has come and brought to our world glorious, comprehensive, faithful, redemptive control. Our talk must flow out of the rest we have found in his rule.

The resources of Christ are our only hope that our words will be spoken up to his standard and according to his design. In the Word we find hope when all seems hopeless, riches when we feel poor, power when we see our weakness, and rule when everything around us seems out of control.

The Gospel and Your Talk

The wholesome talk of the body of Christ at home, church, or work is rooted is the glorious realities of the gospel. The Word has come and brought with him everything we need to live a life of godly talk. Because he has come, we can have hope that our words will follow the pattern of the Great Speaker rather than the Great Deceiver. He has come to deliver us from the horrible damage of the Fall, where the wonderful gift of communication became a terrible world of trouble. Christ has come to tame what man will never tame. He has come to use for his purpose what seems unusable. He has come to endow us with glorious riches and incomparable power so that our tongues can be used as his instruments of righteousness. Our world of talk does not have to be a world of trouble for this one reliable reason: the Word has come.

Getting Personal: Christ and Your Talk

Examine your communication with others this week. Was it built on the solid foundation that Christ has established for us? For example:

1. Do you humbly admit your inability and seek the Lord's help before important times of communication?
2. In your primary relationships, are you seeking to accomplish with words what only the Lord can do by his grace and power?
3. Do you fall prey to hopelessness so that you either give up speaking when your words are needed or give in to patterns of sinful talk?
4. Are you willing to admit your communication weaknesses, recognize recurring themes, confess to God and those you have offended, and commit to new patterns of talk? (All of this is based on embracing Christ's promise that his strength is made perfect in our weakness.)
5. Are you able to humbly consider what others point out as sin in your talk? Or do you deny, rationalize, turn the tables, shift blame, or wallow in your failure?
6. Do you daily thank the Lord for his provision, and the hope it gives that you can speak in a way that blesses others and glorifies him?

Read Ephesians 1:15–23. Ask the Lord to open your eyes to the glorious benefits of Christ's work and the hope it offers for your words. Ask him to show you where change is needed and step out there in faith. Finally, rest in the reality of what John says about the Word: "From the fullness of his grace we have all received one blessing after another" (John 1:16), and believe that his ever-flowing stream of grace can radically change your world of talk.

Chapter Four

Idol Words

Where do you think all these appalling wars and quarrels come from? . . . They come about because you want your own way, and fight for it deep inside yourselves.
(James 4:1–2)

PRETEND with me that it is a weekday morning and I am sitting in my office thinking about my lovely wife. I realize how blessed I am to be married to such a person for so many years. I reflect on the fact that I asked her to marry me when I was seventeen years old! I realize that I didn't have the maturity then to make such a serious decision and that my marriage today is a testimony to the love and grace of the Lord.

As I sit in my office, I also think about how hard it is for Luella and me to have any time alone with each other. We have four children still living at home: two sons who go to college in the city, a daughter in high school, and a son in elementary school. Needless to say, there isn't much quiet around our house! We are way beyond the days when we could put the kids to bed and spend time together. Our children are always still up when we decide to go to bed. In fact, my sons often wake me as I am dozing with the newspaper to ask me why I don't just call it a day. Like my father before me, I instinctively claim that I was not sleeping.

But recently, my son responded that he knew I was sleeping because of the drool on the newspaper!

Anyway, as I am thinking about Luella, being thankful to God for her and bemoaning the pressures of family life that keep us apart, I decide to surprise her that night with dinner out at the restaurant of her choice. I am excited about the idea and I just know that she will be too! When my lunch hour comes around, I run to the local mall to buy her favorite perfume as an expression of my love for her.

As the afternoon progresses, I am more and more taken with the prospect of a night out with my wife. I daydream about the evening to come. In my mind I see it this way: I drive up to the house, leap up the stairs, throw open the front door, and find Luella waiting for me. She says, "Paul, you're finally home! I have been waiting for you. I so look forward to your coming home each afternoon." (You can see whose fantasy this is!) I respond, "I've been thinking all day about how much I love you, and how blessed I am to have you as my wife. And I have a great idea. Let's go out to eat tonight, just the two of us—you pick the restaurant." She responds, "Most of the women I know would love to be married to a man like this!" "Oh, I have another surprise," I say as I pull the perfume out of my pocket. "I bought you your favorite perfume!" "Blessing upon blessing, more than I can contain!" she responds. "I'll go right upstairs and get ready. I can't think of anything I'd rather do than spend an evening with you." The afternoon flies by as my mind keeps replaying the upcoming surprise for my wife.

Now pretend with me that the day is actually over and I am on my way home. By this time, I am fully captivated by the idea of a night out with Luella. I am also fully persuaded that she will think the idea is wonderful too. I sing my way home, not remembering the lights I stopped at or the turns I made. I park in front of the house, bound up the stairs, and throw open the door—but no one is there! Still, my enthusiasm is undiminished.

I walk into the dining room when I hear voices coming from the kitchen. They are not happy voices. In the kitchen I find Luella standing between our two older boys, refereeing an argument. In my excitement, I don't wait for a pause in the action. I just blurt out, "Luella, I've got a great idea!" No one even seems to notice that I have entered the room. I blurt out my announcement again and this time Luella responds, "Did you say something?" "Yes," I say excitedly, "I've been thinking about you all day and I have a great idea. Let's go out to eat tonight, just the two of us. You choose the restaurant and I'll make a reservation while you're getting ready to go."

She looks at me for a moment and responds with a sigh. This is not a positive sign. "Maybe you didn't understand me," I say, trying again. "I want to take you out for a special night at your favorite restaurant, just you and me." Luella sighs again (things are not looking good at all!) and then begins to speak. "Do you know what my day has been like? I feel like I have been the sole peace negotiator in the middle of World War III. I am totally exhausted, physically and mentally. The thought of getting dressed up and going out to a fancy restaurant doesn't seem attractive at all. I do appreciate that you think about me and that you love me, but I have a better idea. Why don't you take the money you were going to use for the restaurant and take the children out for pizza or something? You can have an evening out with the kids and I'll take a long, warm bath and go to bed early."

I can hardly believe what I am hearing. I reply, "God has blessed you with a husband who loves you, a husband who thinks about you, and really wants to be with you, and this is how you respond? Sure, the bath idea is great for you, but what about me? Do you know what happens to the blessings God gives you when you don't properly use them? Do you know how many women would love to be married to a man like me? We will never have the relationship God wants us to have if we both aren't committed to working on it! There seems to be just one thing that we have in common: I am concerned about you and *you* are concerned about you! Sure, I'll take the kids out if that is what you want! We'll take our time. Maybe go and get pizza in Ohio!" (We live in Philadelphia.)

"You enjoy yourself and soak till your skin wrinkles—and, by the way, stick this in the water," I say as I pull out the bottle of perfume. "But you better think about our relationship and how much you are really committed to it."

This (fortunately) fictional situation is all too familiar to most of us. What went wrong? How did an idea born out of thankfulness to God and love for my wife end in such anger and accusation? How did the person who was the focus of my love and appreciation become the target of such anger? What unleashed this flow of blame, guilt manipulation, self-righteousness, and accusation? It is easy to see that the problem here is not just communication technique. I have no trouble making myself heard and using words to advance my point! Something deeper is going on. Let me say it in a phrase and then explain. The problem with my words is that they are *idol words*. No, the spelling is not wrong. Many of our communication problems occur because we are speaking idol words.

Root and Fruit

To understand what I mean, let's look at two passages, beginning with the words of Christ in Luke 6:43–46:

> *No good tree bears bad fruit, nor does a bad tree bear good fruit. Each tree is recognized by its own fruit. People do not pick figs from thornbushes, or grapes from briers. The good man brings good things out of the good stored up in his heart, and the evil man brings evil things out of the evil stored up in his heart. For out of the overflow of his heart his mouth speaks.*

Jesus uses a metaphor with which we all are familiar, a tree. There is an organic connection between the roots of a tree and the fruit it produces. The same is true with our words. They are the fruit of the root issues found in our hearts. Word problems are always related to heart problems. That's why we will not solve communication problems by dealing only with our words, any more than we would solve a problem with a plant's fruit production by dealing only with the fruit. If a plant isn't producing good fruit, there is a problem with the plant system itself, down to its very roots.

Jesus' brilliant metaphor reveals that our words are shaped and controlled by the thoughts and motives of our own hearts. It is very tempting to blame others ("She makes me so angry" or "He pushes all my buttons") or to blame the situation around us ("I just didn't have time to sit down and discuss it calmly," or "With four kids in the house all talking at once, a soft answer just doesn't work"). Christ says that a person's words come "out of the overflow of his heart." In the story that opened this chapter, it was tempting to blame Luella for my self-centered, angry, guilt-inflicting words. I wanted to say that I got upset because she was being selfish, but Christ would say no. Luella did not cause my words. She was simply the occasion, the trigger, for my heart to express itself. My words revealed the true desires of *my* heart.

If we are going to understand our trouble with words, we must begin with the heart. Our tongues are a restless evil *because* the "heart is deceitful above all things and beyond cure. Who can understand it?" (Jer. 17:9). Word problems *reveal* heart problems. The people and situations around us do not *make* us say what we say; they are only the *occasion* for our hearts to reveal themselves in words.

Sue and Jim illustrated this problem as they glared at each other angrily in my office. I had jumped in once again to take control of a conversation that had gone from a simple recounting of the week to a full-blown volley of accusations. This seemed to happen every time they attempted to talk. Did they have serious communication problems? Yes! Are there many biblical principles that relate to the way they talked to one another? Of course! But their inability to have a sane, loving, restrained, and mutually beneficial conversation powerfully revealed the root of their problem. Until they faced what was going on in their hearts, they would not stay inside God's communication boundaries.

I vividly recall the day when Sue said to Jim, "For years I've blamed you for our inability to talk. I've complained to my friends about how hard you are. But God has shown me this week that I have been bitter against you for years. I have kept a record of wrongs and looked with a critical eye at everything you have done. It hit me today that as long as I continue to hate you in my heart, I will not love you with my mouth." This God-given insight led Jim to confess similar sins of his own heart. And in their mutual confession, Jim and Sue laid the foundation for lasting change in their communication.

The problem with the words I spoke to my wife in this chapter's opening story was that they were idol words. They revealed the true love that dominated my heart, and it wasn't Luella—it was myself! An idolatrous heart will produce idol words.

Ruling Desires

What are ruling desires? James 4 can teach us more:

> What causes fights and quarrels among you? Don't they come from your desires that battle within you? You want something but don't get it. You kill and covet, but you cannot have what you want. You quarrel and fight. You do not have, because you do not ask God. When you ask, you do not receive, because you ask with wrong motives, that you may spend what you get on your pleasures.
>
> You adulterous people, don't you know that friendship with the world is hatred toward God? Anyone who chooses to be a friend of the world becomes an enemy of God. Or do you think that Scripture says without reason that the spirit he caused to live in us envies intensely? But he gives us more grace. That is why Scripture says:

"God opposes the proud
but gives grace to the humble."

Submit yourselves, then, to God. Resist the devil, and he
will flee from you. Come near to God and he will come near
to you. Wash your hands, you sinners, and purify your
hearts, you double-minded. Grieve, mourn and wail. Change
your laughter to mourning and your joy to gloom. Humble
yourselves before the Lord, and he will lift you up. (vv. 1–10)

When James asks why we speak quarrelsome words, or why
we are better at making war than we are at making peace, he
does not answer the questions this way: "What causes fights and
quarrels among you? *Don't they come from your lack of skill in conflict*
resolution? You want to avoid conflicts, but you haven't learned the
strategies and techniques to be successful at it." No, James goes in a
radically different direction. He directs us to examine the desires
of *our own hearts.* What I speak is directly related to what I want.
My words are one means I use to get what is important to me.

Let's look again at the specific words of this passage. James
says, "Don't they [quarrels and fights] come from your desires
that battle within you? You want something but you don't get
it." According to James, quarrels are caused by desires battling
within our hearts. Now, we need to be careful here. James does
not say it is wrong for us to *desire.* When you quit desiring, you
are seriously deceased! We will always desire something. Notice
also that James does not say that the problem is *evil* desires, that
is, that we are desiring things that are bad in and of themselves.

Think back on the story of my desire to spend an evening
with my wife. The problem was not that I desired her. That desire was natural, good, and healthy. Nor was the problem that
I had some kind of evil desire toward my wife. The original desire to be with her was born out of heartfelt appreciation for
her and thankfulness to God. James is not saying that it is
wrong to desire or that our problem is that we are desiring
bad things. What then *is* the problem?

The answer is found in this important phrase: "They come from your desires *that battle* within you." There is a war going on within our hearts, a war for control. James is saying that when a certain set of desires battles for "turf" in our hearts, it will affect the way we deal with the people around us. Whatever controls our hearts will control our words. In fact, you could argue that if a certain desire controls my heart, there are only two ways I can respond to you. If you help me get what I want, I will enjoy and appreciate you. But if you stand in my way, I will experience (and probably express) anger when you are around. I want something, but because of you I cannot get it, so I will quarrel and fight!

In our story something very important happened to me during the day. A good desire for time with my wife waged war in my heart *until it had taken control.* Personal desires battled for the authority that *only God* should exercise over my heart. When God no longer functionally ruled my heart, the desire took on a new character. By the time I reached the house, the desire that motivated me was no longer an expression of love for Luella and worship of God. No, it had become an expression of self-love. I no longer was looking for a way to serve Luella, to communicate my love and appreciation for her. Rather, I wanted to possess her for the evening for my own pleasure! The problem is that I did not see that the original desire had "morphed" into something very different.

If I had been, in fact, motivated by love for Luella, I would have had a wonderful opportunity to express that love by giving her a quiet evening of relaxation. And I would have had a wonderful opportunity to serve God by teaching my children, by example, to look for ways to love their neighbor as themselves. But I was no longer seeking to express my love and appreciation for Luella. I wanted her for myself and I would not let her say no. The desire had become a demand. At that moment it effectively replaced God as the controller of my heart. Scripture calls this an idol. Idolatry is when my heart is controlled or ruled by anything other than God.

This happens to us more than we would tend to think. The desire for success at work becomes a demand for appreciation from the boss. The desire to have enough money to pay the bills morphs into a lust for affluence. The desire to be a good parent becomes a desire to have children who enhance my reputation. The desire for friendship becomes a demand to be accepted and anger when I'm not. What was once a healthy desire *takes control,* and when this happens, the desire that originally motivated me changes into something very different. Rather than being motivated by a love for God and my neighbor, I am motivated by a pursuit of what will bring me pleasure, and I am angry at anyone who stands in the way.

The Elevation of Desire

An idolatrous heart will produce idol words, words that serve the idol that grips us. It is hard for us to hold our desires loosely. Instead, they tend to take hold of us. Our desires tend to get elevated to a position where they should never be. Here is what happens: A *desire* battles for control until it becomes a *demand.* The *demand* is then expressed (and usually experienced) as a *need.* ("I need sex." "I need respect.") My sense of *need* sets up my *expectation. Expectation* when unfulfilled leads to *disappointment. Disappointment* leads to some kind of *punishment.* "You want something, but you cannot get it. You quarrel and fight." So when James says, "You adulterous people," he is not changing the subject. He is saying something very significant. Adultery takes place when I give the love I have promised one person to someone else. Spiritual adultery occurs when I give the love that belongs to God alone to something or someone else. James is saying that *human conflict is rooted in spiritual adultery!* This is what had happened in my heart as I planned out the evening. This is a momentous thought! We will not solve our problem with angry words until we humbly address the adultery and idolatry of our hearts.

James has upped the ante here. Perhaps this does not seem comforting, but by so doing he shows us the only solution that *really* goes to the heart of the problem. The promise of the gospel extends deeper than new techniques and strategies. It aims at more than a temporary lull in the storm of words. The gospel holds out the promise of nothing less than a new heart, one that is no longer enslaved to the passions and desires of the sinful nature. So, for Jim and Sue, for Paul and Luella, there is hope for real and lasting change.

How does this change begin? We need to heed James's words again as he says, "Submit yourselves, then, to God." Change begins at the level of the heart. We must renounce the idols that have replaced God and turn our hearts back to him, so that our words will reflect a heart ruled by God alone. For James, this change is seen on two levels. We must "wash our hands," that is, there must be change in our behavior. The words we say, the way we say them, and when they are said all must be changed where necessary, but that is not enough. James also says, "Purify your hearts." Change must include our thoughts and motives as well. We need change both in the content and manner of our talk and in what effectively controls our hearts.

The Great Exchange

By the time I arrived in the kitchen on that imaginary afternoon, a significant exchange had taken place. Without realizing it, I had exchanged thankfulness to God and love for my wife for a worship of self and a demand that my wife serve me. I entered the room unwilling to live without that evening with my wife. I no longer had a loosely held, God-honoring desire, but a demand that had grown to a sense of need. I fully expected Luella to support my idea and run upstairs to get ready. In the face of her disagreement, I immediately got angry at her and did everything I could to get her to yield to my wishes. The person who had been the object of my affection was now the focus of my anger. She hadn't caused my anger—it flowed out of my own idolatrous desires. Again, those desires were not intrinsically evil. But when they became ruling desires, they replaced God as the ruler of my heart. Though my words were selfish, angry, and manipulative, the more serious problem was that they were idolatrous.

Romans 1 brings this issue to clearer focus for us: "They exchanged the truth of God for a lie, and worshiped and served created things rather than the Creator—who is forever praised. Amen" (v. 25).

The operative word of this passage is "*exchanged.*" This is fundamentally what sin is all about. In the heart of every sinner is a tendency to exchange worship and service of the Creator for worship and service of the created thing. All human beings are worshippers; the issue is only what or whom we worship. Idolatry gives the worship that belongs to God to some aspect of his creation. It might be a craving for human love, respect, appreciation, or applause. It might be a certain person, position, economic state, or living situation. There is no end to the created things that can replace God as the object of our worship.

There is a constant migration in the heart of every sinner away from the worship and service of God toward the worship and service of some aspect of the creation. It can be a lifelong migration—that is, a theme of heart idolatry can characterize a person's whole life—or it can be more spontaneous and short-term, as in the story we've been considering. In this case, a desire takes control for a few hours, but still wreaks havoc.

Putting Communication in the Right Drawer

What we are considering is the bottom line on the war of words. The Scriptures tell us that if we are ever going to see lasting change in our communication, we must start from within. Only as we deal with the idolatry of our hearts will we be freed from speaking idol words. As we said in the first chapter, God is the Lord and Creator of human language. All of our words must be spoken according to his purpose and for his glory. To do anything less is idolatry.

One final piece of biblical wisdom will help us here. The Pharisees tried to ensnare Christ by asking him which was the greatest command in the law. His answer is one of the most significant passages in all of Scripture (see Matt. 22:37–40). Christ says you can boil all of the teaching of Scripture down to two areas: love for God and love for people, and he says something else important. There is an *order* of importance here: love for God is foundational to everything else. If you do not love God above all else, you will not love your neighbor as yourself. Any lack of love for neighbor, in word or deed, reflects some deficiency in your love for God (see 1 John 4:7–21). This is why James says that human conflict is rooted in spiritual adultery.

Jesus' statement addresses one of the principal mistakes the church tends to make when it deals with the subject of communication. Christ says that there are two drawers in God's filing cabinet: drawer one is entitled "Love for God" and drawer two is entitled "Love for Neighbor." Everything Scripture teaches can be filed in one of these drawers. Our mistake has been to treat the issue of communication as if it were a drawer two issue exclusively. When we deal with communication problems in marriage and family, in parenting, friendship, community, and the body of Christ, too often we immediately turn to the scriptural commands and principles that speak to this topic without examining the passages that address the heart behind the principles. In so doing, we neglect the heart issues that must be addressed if these passages are to be obeyed. Words that are spoken up to God's standard and according to his design always begin with a heart that loves God above all else, and therefore desires to speak in a loving way to one's neighbor.

Communication is both a drawer one and drawer two issue.

If we do not deal with what we really love, with what really rules our hearts, we will never be able to speak to one another in the way God has called us to speak. We must start with the heart, because as Christ said in Luke 6, it is out of the overflow of our hearts that our mouths speak. As James has said, we fight and quarrel because of the desires that have taken control there. Our words are one of the ways we seek to gain, maintain, and keep what is really important to us, what we really want, and what we are really living for. If idol words are going to turn into God-honoring words, we must begin by humbly examining our hearts. What or whom are we really serving?

How are you feeling as you read this? Perhaps you are thinking, *Great, Paul, I started out with one problem and now I've got two! I've never seen these angry, quarrelsome words as something against God. This is really discouraging!* But don't be discouraged. God never reveals our hearts to discourage us. Convicting us of sin is one of the most profound ways he demonstrates his love for us. He is committed to completing his work in us. He will not allow us to live with hearts that are enslaved. He works in every situation so that we would know the freedom his death purchased for us. So, he exposes not only the fruit of our sin (wrong words), but the roots of our sin (heart idols) as well. The conviction of our hearts is a sign that we are his dearly loved children, who have not only been forgiven of our sins, but are in the process of being delivered from them.

Don't be discouraged! Your Redeemer has come. He is battling on your behalf in every situation, in each relationship, so that you can win the war of words.

Getting Personal: Getting to the Heart of Communication Problems

In what ways do you tend to blame your communication problems on things outside yourself? (In this fallen world there will always be plenty of ways to shift blame!)

1. Do you tend to blame your negative communication on *situations*?
   - traffic
   - schedule
   - finances
   - weather
   - vehicle
   - job
   - family
   - extended family
2. Do you tend to blame *others*?
   - wife
   - husband
   - children
   - parents
   - boss
   - co-workers
   - body of Christ
3. Do you tend to blame God? "If only I had . . ."
   - more money
   - a more understanding spouse
   - a better education
   - a more understanding pastor/church
   - more obedient children
   - a more loving, supportive extended family
   - better neighbors
   - a more reasonable boss

Examine your heart with hope, remembering that "if we confess our sins, he is faithful and just and will forgive us our sins and purify us from all unrighteousness" (1 John 1:9).

(part two)

a new agenda for our talk

Listen for God's voice in everything you do,
everywhere you go; he's the one who will
keep you on track. (Prov. 3:6)

O God, I have stood
* in the shadow of mountains,*
* at the brink of oceans,*
* under the spread of clouds,*
* by the foot of redwoods—*
And I have learned of Your greatness.
O Lord, I have touched
* baby fingers,*
* feathers of a canary,*
* petals of a rose,*
* lather from soap—*
And I have been reminded of Your gentleness.
O Father, I have known
* true friendship,*
* joys of love,*
* unconcerned care,*
* unrestricted consideration—*
And I have thought of Your goodness.
O great, gentle, good God,
* do some good, gentle, great thing*
* today through me,*
* that others too may know*
* more of You,*
*   I pray,*
*   In Christ's Name,*
*   Amen.*

Chapter Five

He Is King!

He is in charge of it all, has the final word on everything. . . . No name and no power [are] exempt from his rule. (Eph. 1:21–22)

HAVE you ever felt as if your brain was so full that one more thought would cause it to explode? I felt that way while standing in a slum in New Delhi, India. I was there to see the work of the mission leaders I had come to India to train. The experiences of the previous few days had filled my mind to the point of overload. The sun was brightly shining and children were playing in the street, but this was not like home. I was overwhelmed by the desperate poverty I was viewing; I still have trouble adequately describing it. I was overwhelmed by the spiritual darkness—so great, so deep, and so pervasive that it seemed like a cloud hanging over us.

I had seen hungry mothers hold sick, starving, fly-infested children. I had seen old beggars who had known few moments of life without physical suffering and need. I had seen places called homes that I wouldn't have used to store a lawn mower. I had seen a handsome, intellectual, young priest prostrate himself before a wooden idol. I had heard a guru defend his seventeen-year quest for enlightenment, an enlightenment he admitted hadn't happened and didn't appear close. I had been moved to see little ten- and eleven-year-old boys a thousand miles from home, already living in an ashram. I was touched to see a family who had traveled for four hundred miles, mostly by foot, to reach a holy place where they could do homage to the gods.

My brain was full—not just full with the sights and experiences, but with a recognition of the vast difference between the lives I was viewing and my own. On the one hand, it was apparent that these were people just like me. They laughed, they cried, they had hopes and dreams, they had families, friends, and homes of a sort. There were things they believed and things they did not. Each day they got up with places to go and things to do. Yet at the same time, our lives were so completely different that we seemed to be from totally different universes. Then, as I stood in that slum on that sunny morning, it hit me. There was only one explanation for the vast differences in our lives—God. That was it, and nothing else!

I don't know when I have been more powerfully aware of the absolute sovereignty of God than I was at that moment. There was no other possible explanation. The choice of birthplace, family, and living conditions all were his. I could have been born in that slum! It wasn't because of *my* wisdom that I was born in Toledo, Ohio! That was the choice of a sovereign God. The choice of who comes to understand truth and who will embrace falsehood belongs to God and God alone. I could have been that young priest. He was not there because he was stupid. It was God who allowed me to be born into a family of faith, who planned that at nine years old I would be convicted by the words of Romans 3, and that I would have the opportunity to spend my life, not worshipping a wooden image, but studying and teaching the Word of God. The words of Romans 11:33–36 flooded into my mind:

> *Oh, the depth of the riches of the wisdom and knowledge of*
> *God!*
> *How unsearchable his judgments,*
> *and his paths beyond tracing out!*

"Who has known the mind of the Lord?
Or who has been his counselor?"
"Who has ever given to God,
that God should repay him?"
For from him and through him and to him are all things.
To him be the glory forever! Amen.

You may be wondering what all this has to do with communication. My answer is that a life of godly communication is rooted in a personal recognition of the sovereignty of God. Let me put it this way: Only when I submit to the rule of God, who has a *perfect plan* and is in *complete control,* will I begin to live and speak as he has purposed. Only at this level will the idolatry of heart that leads to idol words be broken. Here alone will my words be freed from being the tools of *my* agenda, *my* attempts at control, and *my* glory-seeking.

When my heart is more controlled by a desire for the creation (a person, possession, position, or experience) than it is by a desire for the Creator, I will seek to control my world (and the people in it) to get what I want. The teenager yells at his parents who have said no to him, "I can't stand you and your rules." The husband who wants his way argues his wife into a corner. The wife seeks to motivate her husband with guilt. The manipulator uses flattery to get what he wants from his friend. None rests in God's sovereignty, believing that he will give what is best.

But when we understand God's sovereignty and submit to his rule, we can live and speak as God has designed. This is the polar opposite of living and speaking *according to our plan, for our control, and for our own glory.* Such self-interest is what brought so much trouble to our talk. The war of words is, at bottom, a war for sovereignty.

Maybe this is why fantasy is such a universal temptation. When I fantasize, I go to worlds of my own making where I rule as absolute sovereign. Every person does my bidding. Every situation unfolds according to my will. In my mind, I function as God and rule unchallenged. *This* world exists for my pleasure and operates exactly as I wish. Fantasy can be one way we fulfill a heart's desire to be lord over our circumstances and relationships.

This struggle for lordship is also revealed in our communication. God's will is that all of our speaking be done for the praise of *his* glory—an exciting new agenda very different from our own. For this reason it is important to understand what the Bible teaches about God's sovereignty. It is the cornerstone for a new agenda for our words.

In talking about this doctrine, I know that I am raising thorny issues that go beyond the scope of typical communication discussions. The connections with the way we talk may not be immediately apparent. But I urge you to stay with me, because I believe that this is one of the reasons we have so many communication problems in the first place! We live in a church culture that tends to separate biblical commands and principles from the rest of Scripture. We look at specific verses about communication and seek to apply them to our lives without understanding the way they are rooted in the history and theology of Scripture. We miss the big picture—the way the rest of Scripture gives these commands their meaning and rationale. The commands and principles of Scripture flow from the theology of Scripture. More than that, they find their hope and meaning in the person and work of Christ.

For example, the only reason it makes sense to do good to your enemies is that the One who has told us to is a God of perfect justice. The call to forgive is rooted in the fact that Christ has forgiven us. The call to give sacrificially is rooted in God's promise to provide for all our needs. Every command and principle has its roots in redemptive realities—what God has done and will do for us in Christ. This is theology—but it's certainly not abstract information! Scripture is full of theology because when you understand truth about God, you understand *why* and *how* you are to carry out the commands of Scripture. You understand how your actions connect with what God is doing, and how you can actually bring glory to his name.

Understanding God's Sovereignty

So, what does the Bible teach about God's sovereign rule? We need to understand this important doctrine because the roots of biblical communication grow in the soil of his sovereignty. If my words don't flow out of a heart that rests in his control, then they come out of a heart that seeks control, so I can get what I want. I need a better understanding of what God is doing.

When the Bible talks of God's sovereignty, it means the following:

1. *His unchallenged rule of the universe.* God is the Lord of Lords and the King of Kings. He has no peer; he not only is Lord over every ruler on earth, but he is also Lord of the heavens. The entire universe operates according to his good pleasure. No one has taught God, no one gives him advice, no one can legitimately question him, and no one can stand in the way of his will. He sits on the throne of the universe, and he alone rules.

This truth is captured in words spoken by Nebuchadnezzar, after God restored him to his sanity.

> *His dominion is an eternal dominion;*
> *his kingdom endures from generation to generation.*
> *All the peoples of earth*
> *are regarded as nothing.*
> *He does as he pleases*
> *with the powers of heaven*
> *and the peoples of the earth.*
> *No one can hold back his hand*
> *or say to him: "What have you done?" (Dan. 4:34–35)*

Now, what does all this mean for my communication? For one thing, it means that I will never be in a situation, location, or relationship in which God is not ruling. The moments of life are *his* moments; I should not claim them as my own. Every word I speak should acknowledge his control. My job is not to get what pleases me, to establish power or to seek control. My job is to submit to God's rule and to do his will. When it comes to communication, my job is to speak in a way that pleases the One who is ruling the very moment in which I am speaking.

When I know that God is in control of my life, I do not give in to panic. I do not begin thinking that life is out of control, and I do not despair when I am confused about what is going on. I know that every situation is under the careful administration of the King of Kings. As I grab hold of this truth by faith, I can pay attention to what God has called me to do—to live and speak in a way that brings him glory.

2. *God rules over all things for the church.* God's rule has a direction and purpose to it: it is for the redemptive benefit of his people. He created everything that is; he has ruled over every moment of human history; he breathed life into dust to make man in his image; he has raised up rulers and nations and has cast them down; he has harnessed the forces of nature; he has raised up his prophets, judges, kings, and apostles; he has revealed himself in a myriad of ways; he has sent his Son to live on earth and to die a criminal's death; he has given us his Word; he rules over our individual lives; and he is coming again. Why? To raise up a people for his own possession (1 Peter 2:9), a people who have been called out of darkness into his marvelous light to live for eternity for his glory! He rules for the sake of his people—for us.

However, to say that God rules for our sake does not mean that he rules so that we can get what we want. No, his rule is redemptive. That is, he controls the universe so that his redemptive purpose *for* us and his redemptive promises *to* us will be fulfilled. He rules so that the justification, sanctification, and glorification he promises us are guaranteed. To that end, the Messiah came, invaded the kingdom of darkness, and led out his people to live for his glory in the kingdom of light (Col. 1:9–14). To guarantee this, God has ruled over all things from eternity past and will continue throughout eternity future. Paul says this of Christ:

> *[He] seated him at his right hand in the heavenly realms, far above all rule and authority, power and dominion, and every title that can be given, not only in the present age but also in the one to come. And God placed all things under his feet and appointed him to be head over everything for the church, which is his body, the fullness of him who fills everything in every way. (Eph. 1:20–22)*

If we get hold of this truth, how will it change the way we speak with one another? Think about how much of our communication involves complaining about our circumstances: our bills, tough neighbors, difficult job, rebellious children, distant husband, unappreciative wife, ineffective church leaders, defective lawn mower, broken-down car, heavy taxes, college tuition, and inability to afford a "good" vacation.

How much of our speaking expresses irritation toward people who get in our way? Family members who rob us of our peace and quiet or who tear up the newspaper before we read it? The rebellious child who robs us of our comfort and ease? The family member who stands in the way of an evening out? The person who refuses to give me the respect and admiration I think I deserve? The person who blocks my promotion at work? The daughter or son who is in the bathroom when I need to be? The wife who never makes my favorite meals or thanks me when I hand her the grocery money? The teenager who never seems happy or content? The pastor who never asks me to do anything significant in the church? The list goes on and on.

So much of our talk expresses envy toward others who seem to have it easier than we do: the non-Christian neighbor who used bonus money to build an addition on his house; the Christian friend who seems to be the particular object of God's blessing; the friend whose son just got a full scholarship to an Ivy League college; the brother in Christ who has had white-collar job security for years; the friend who has a happy and vivacious wife or warm, loving husband; the unbelieving friend who never has trouble paying his bills and seems to have great kids; the factory worker who just won the lottery.

So much of our praise to the Lord is limited to the moments when *we* have determined that what he has done is good: the times of physical healing, financial provision, improved circumstances, restored relationships, or solved problems. In these situations, we praise God for his faithfulness.

But what does all of this communication miss? The fact that God is active in *every* moment of our lives, and that he brings *all* things into our lives for our redemptive good. It is very, very important that we believe this! When we do, we have hearts that can speak with humility and worship. We realize that God has us just where we need to be so that his purposes for us and his promises to us may come to pass.

3. *God rules over the specific details of our lives.* God's rule is not just global or universal, it is individual. We see this played out in the lives of familiar characters in Scripture. He is Lord over the details of the lives of Moses, Jacob and Esau, Joseph, Esther, Ruth, David, Jeremiah, Daniel, Peter, and Paul, to name but a few. He rules ours as well. His rule actually includes the details of the lives of every human being who ever lived! The glory of this is too much for our minds to grasp. We have trouble organizing our own lives! But God is so glorious in his sovereignty that he directs the specific details of every human life at the same time.

Paul spoke of this in the Areopagus as he introduced the

people of Athens to the God they knew as "Unknown": *"He determined the times set for them and the exact places where they should live"* (Acts 17:26).

God's rule is not distant and impersonal. Just the opposite! God rules over the specifics of my life so that I can reach out and find him (see v. 27). He calls us to think, pray, and plan and to live ordered and self-controlled lives, but on a foundation that recognizes and rests in his rule.

Maybe you have communication problems over things *you* think are problems, but God does not. We often focus on people and situations, while God's focus is on us. He is using the things in our lives as tools for accomplishing his work in us.

4. *God rules over every aspect of our salvation.* This has been the most controversial aspect of God's rule in the church, yet it is clearly proclaimed in Scripture and is the basis for the security of every believer. Here the final vestiges of our reliance on human power, performance, goodness, and self-sufficiency are laid waste. True worship begins as we grasp the sovereign grace of God. Our salvation exists on the rock of his will. Even the first breath of our faith has been determined by him before the foundations of the world. Without his love placed upon us, we would be excluded from the citizenship of his people, separate from his covenant promises, without hope and without God in the world (Eph. 2:12)!

God opens spiritual eyes that we may see and spiritual ears that we may hear (see Matt. 13:11–17; John 10:25–30). Every aspect of our salvation depends on him. There is no clearer statement of this truth than from Paul:

> *For he chose us in him before the creation of the world to be holy and blameless in his sight. In love he predestined us to be adopted as his sons through Jesus Christ, in accordance with his pleasure and will—to the praise of his glorious grace, which he has freely given us in the One he loves. (Eph. 1:4–6)*

What is God's purpose in his sovereignty over our salvation? It is twofold. First, God's sovereign grace undermines all human pride and thoughts of self-sufficiency as we face our complete dependence on him. If there is *any* spiritual life, faith, goodness, love, hope, grace, character, wisdom, and God-honoring fruit in our lives, it is because of God's grace. We are what we are because of him.

Second, God's goal is that the pride we would otherwise have in ourselves be given over to praising him. Paul says, "Let him who boasts boast in the Lord" (1 Cor. 1:31). Notice the phrase that is repeated in Ephesians 1—"to the praise of his glory." This is what God had in mind: That his rule over every aspect of our salvation would result in an eternal chorus of praise.

This is the bottom line of biblical communication, the first and highest goal of all of our talk: that our words would reflect an attitude of worship that recognizes our utter dependency on God for salvation. He has chosen us to be his children, he called us to himself, he breathed life into us so that we could see and believe the truth, he justified us and adopted us into his family, he daily works to sanctify us, and he will take us to glory. It is all of him. Out of that realization will come a life of communication that benefits others and honors him.

The fact is that our words always express worship—but not always of God. We've seen that we tend to exchange worship and service of the Creator for worship and service of the created thing (Rom. 1:25). We see it in the wife who says, "Don't tell me how much God loves me. I want a husband who loves me!" We hear it from the teenager who says, "I hate living here. I can never do what I want to do!" It's even evident in the toddler who throws a tantrum in the toy store because Mom refused to buy him a ball. The pastor says, "Why do I try to minister to these people? All I ever get is criticism." The employee says, "All I want from my job is a raise and a little credit."

In every case, each statement is motivated more by worship and service of the creation than it is by worship and service of the Creator. God desires to redirect our focus.

5. *God rules over circumstances for our sanctification.* There is probably no more important perspective on our everyday life than this: God is at work in every situation to conform us to the image of his Son. This truth is presented all over the New Testament (see Rom. 8:28–29; James 1:2–4; 1 Peter 1:3–9).

Each passage says essentially the same thing: that God is at work to complete the work of salvation he began before the earth was made. Paul says he is working in all things for the good of conforming us to the image of his Son. James says we ought to greet trials with joy because God is using them to complete us. Peter says we can view trials as the means by which we receive the goal of our faith, the salvation of our souls. God is sovereign over the circumstances of our lives, but Scripture says more. It tells us that these circumstances are a principal means by which God actually produces what he predestined for our lives before the foundation of the world—that we would be transformed into the likeness of his Son, holy as he is holy.

When we complain about the problems and pressures in our lives, we are essentially grumbling in the face of God. We are complaining that we have been chosen by his love and grace, and that he is putting us in situations designed to make us his holy people! These relationships and circumstances, these problems and trials, and these times of grief and suffering come from his hand. They are tokens of God's wonderful grace, given to deliver us from the power of remaining sin! Behind the circumstances is a God of love who is relentlessly at work to make us holy. Praise that comes from hearts of worship is the only legitimate response to these circumstances. Rather than telling us that God has forgotten us, our circumstances shout to us that he has remembered us and will not leave us until his work is complete! Really understanding this will do much to alter the way we talk.

For example, I am a very schedule-oriented person. I awake every day with an agenda. I try to do everything quickly. I tend to evaluate the success of a day by how many things I got done. So it is very easy for me to get frustrated when my day doesn't work out as I had planned. I find myself increasingly frustrated with things ("Stupid computer!"), with people ("Why isn't he here? Doesn't he know how busy I am?"), and with situations ("Why does the whole world decide to get office supplies just when I need a refill for my pen?"). In all of this I tend to forget that God is focused not on the "success" of my day but on the godliness of my character. I tend to focus on the results. He is committed to the process of making me holy. In my anger and frustration, I am not just fighting people and situations, but God.

What comes out of your mouth in times of trouble? What does your heart think and your mouth say when your plan is obstructed or simply falls flat? How do you respond when people fail you or don't do their part? What do you say in moments of frustration and disappointment? How do you respond when you face the totally unexpected? How do you react toward those who seem to stand in the way of your schedule and plans? How do you respond when your brightest ideas and best efforts fall apart? How do you react to trials that don't seem to be your fault? Do your words acknowledge the sovereign plan of God over all of your circumstances for your sanctification?

The New Testament writers tell us that we should not be surprised when we face trouble, trial, and suffering. They tell us that we should never conclude that God has forgotten us. They say that for the believer, the opposite is true: trials are the result of his covenant love! We experience difficulty precisely *because* we are the children of his love. God will not neglect us so that we can experience the ease we want. No, he will perfect us through trial after trial.

God's people have always struggled with this truth. When Israel was trapped at the Red Sea with the Egyptians closing in behind them, Exodus 13 tells us that their situation was not an accident or the result of poor planning on Moses' part. It was the plan and provision of God. Israel could have taken a much shorter route to Palestine, but God knew that they were not spiritually ready. Moses records it this way: "For God said, 'If they face war, they might change their minds and return to Egypt'" (v. 17). God led them a different way until they were camped at the Red Sea. Not only that, but God hardened Pharaoh's heart so that he would pursue them (Ex. 14:1–4). Why? Moses records God's answer: "'But I will gain glory for myself through Pharaoh and all his army, and the Egyptians will know that I am the LORD'" (v. 4). God was in control of the whole circumstance, strengthening his people for the battles they would face in the Promised Land.

How did the people respond?

> As Pharaoh approached, the Israelites looked up, and there were the Egyptians, marching after them. They were terrified and cried out to the LORD. They said to Moses, "Was it because there were no graves in Egypt that you brought us to the desert to die? What have you done to us by bringing us out of Egypt? Didn't we say to you in Egypt, 'Leave us alone; let us serve the Egyptians'? It would have been better for us to serve the Egyptians than to die in the desert!" (vv. 10–12)

Isn't this a typical human reaction? You can hear the Israelites asking each other, "Did you vote for Moses?" or saying, "We should have known—he was already a failure. . . . It was obvious that he was going to get us into a mess!" There seems to be no awareness that Israel was brought into the circumstance by God. He had them just where he wanted them to receive what he wanted to give them. It should have been obvious that this was not Moses' fault because Israel had been led by the pillar of cloud by day and the pillar of fire by night (Ex. 13:20–22)—a visible indicator that they had been brought to the Red Sea by the Lord. Yet, in their panic, they forgot the

Lord and his sovereign plan. Instead, they blamed and accused their human leader.

Notice that this trial produced *exactly* what God had planned for his people. "And when the Israelites saw the great power the LORD displayed against the Egyptians, the people feared the LORD and put their trust in him and in Moses his servant" (Ex. 14:31). Paul says that these incidents are examples and warnings for us (1 Cor. 10:11). They reveal our hearts and expose our reactions to trial. We, too, forget the presence of a sovereign God and curse our situation and blame the people around us. God wants us to remember the truth of his sanctifying control over our circumstances. This is the only way to build a biblical model of communication.

The tough neighbor, demanding boss, touchy relative, controlling friend, unthankful child, and the unexpected accident are all tools of sanctification in the hands of our Lord. Like you, I have trouble interpreting them properly. I tend to see them as signs that God has forgotten me rather than sure indications that he is near, carefully controlling things for my good. So I fret and complain instead of resting and worshipping.

6. *God rules over relationships for my sanctification.* The people in my life are not there by accident. They, too, are instruments in the hands of my Redeemer. Through them he continues the work he has begun in me. This is powerfully depicted as Paul talks about the church (see Eph. 2:14–16, 19–22; 4:16; 1 Cor. 12:12–13, 18–20, 27).

God is sovereign over my relationships. He has placed the stones in the temple just where he wanted them. He has arranged every part of the body as he wanted it to be. These relationships are a means by which God continues his work. The struggles they bring are not meaningless hassles or irritating obstacles to an otherwise happy life. No, they are there because God is covenantally committed to bring us to maturity, to "attaining to the whole measure of the fullness of Christ" (Eph. 4:12).

I was a young pastor when, one Sunday morning, I was

asked by a man in our congregation if he could talk with me on Monday. I was excited. I thought, *Finally someone has been touched by my ministry and is seeking my counsel!* Little did I know what I was facing. We got together on Monday night and he said to me, "Paul, I didn't come here to talk about me. I want to talk about you." (Not exactly what I had anticipated!) During the next two hours, he took apart every aspect of my ministry, and my person as well. I was devastated. I thought I couldn't feel any worse until he suggested that we go to his house so I could talk with his wife. For an hour and a half she echoed her husband's sentiments.

I don't know when I have felt so wronged or so wounded. I told Luella that I didn't want to quit the ministry, I wanted to die! I called my brother, Tedd, wanting him to dress my wounds. I wanted him to tell me what a good guy I was and how I didn't have to listen to this awful couple. But he told me just the opposite. Tedd said, "Pay careful attention, Paul. God had you in that room for a reason. Whatever evil they meant is not nearly as important as the good that God is trying to do in all of this."

Boy, I didn't want to hear those words! I wanted to say to Tedd, "Are you nuts? How can this be good? I've tried my best to serve God and this is what I get?!" But I did listen, and as the hurt passed, God began to show me attitudes and actions that were hindering the work he wanted to do through me. I can say now that I am very thankful for that painful Monday night. God used it to change my life and my ministry.

How often do we forget this truth when we speak to (and about) the people in our lives? How often do we treat people as irritants and obstacles? How frequently do we lash out against them in anger because they stand in the way of our plans or our momentary happiness? How often do we complain to others about their actions, reactions, and words? How much do we bemoan the fact that our lives are affected by others' choices? Embracing the sovereignty of God over our relationships will alter our words regarding the people he has placed in our lives.

7. *God rules over all things for* his *glory.* This is the bottom line of everything Scripture says about the sovereignty of God. He does what he does for his own glory. History *is* his story. Every moment belongs to him. We are his possessions. All of our gifts, graces, and abilities belong to him. It is all from him, all for him, and as Paul says three times in Ephesians 1, all for "the praise of his glory."

God is not working for our temporal personal happiness. He is not working so that we would feel satisfied and complete or that we would have a positive self-image or a comfortable lifestyle. No, he is working to make us lights that shine in darkness, so that people would see our good works and give him glory (Matt. 5:16). People who grasp this truth shine like "a city on a hill" that "cannot be hidden" (v. 14).

This is why God teaches us again and again in Scripture that our lives are in his hands. All human boasting should give way to the ultimate purpose of his own glory. When we speak as if we are in control (or ought to be), when we take glory for ourselves, when we complain about the things God has put on our plate, we are rejecting his ultimate purpose for us—that we would be people who live (and speak) for his glory. With James we need to admit, "Out of the same mouth come praise and cursing. My brothers, this should not be" (James 3:10).

In light of this, every word we speak must meet two standards. First, all of our words should bring God the glory he deserves. And second, our words should bring redemptive good into the lives of the people God has placed around us. This is a high calling for all our words—worship and redemption. But this is also why there is a great war of words, for the Enemy fights to keep us from fulfilling this calling. The Deceiver wants us to claim the world of words as our own, to speak out of our *own* will, to speak for our *own* glory, and to speak out of selfish hearts committed only to what seems best for *us*. Here again, the war of words is really a war for sovereignty. Whatever or whoever rules our hearts will control the words we speak. The clear message of Scripture is that we are called to speak out of a thankful heart of submission to God, in every circumstance and situation.

Do you have a better idea of what the sovereignty of God has to do with our speaking? It is the foundation for a new agenda. Only as I submit to the rule of the Lord will I begin to live and speak as he purposed. Only then am I freed to speak in an attitude of worship and as an instrument of redemption, leaving the things I can't understand or control to his unsearchable knowledge, wisdom, and sovereign choice.

As I wrote this chapter, I was privileged to be part of a sad but powerful experience. My father-in-law was taken to the hospital with an advanced case of bone cancer. He lay in bed in severe pain, yet he was not angry. He did not complain or ask, "Why me?" My wife stood at the end of his bed watching this once-strong man lie frail and broken. At the end of our visit he asked if he could pray. It was a prayer we will never forget. The first thing he did was to thank God for his circumstances. He said that he knew that God was good and that everything he did in his children's lives was good even when we don't understand it. Then he asked God to help him be a good father and a good example to his children during his suffering. He finally thanked God for the rich life of blessings he had been given.

This man was not a theologian. There had been a time when I struggled to respect him because he did not seem to understand truths I thought I had mastered in seminary. I have since come to realize that his life demonstrated a grasp of God's sovereignty that I do not have. I long to have such rest in the midst of trouble! I long for my talk to be as wholesome, edifying, and worshipful as his was. I no longer struggle to respect my father-in-law. I would be very thankful if my sons turned out to be like him. Bert Jackson won the war of words because the war for sovereignty had been won in his heart. In the moment of his great suffering, his talk encouraged and strengthened the people around him and brought glory to God. Why? Because he really did believe, when the rubber met the road, that God has a perfect plan and is in complete control. He really did want everything he did and said to bring God glory, and he did not think that personal suffering excused him from that high calling.

The war of words is really a war for sovereignty. Who or what rules your heart? Whoever or whatever it is, it will control your tongue as well.

Getting Personal: The Battle for Control

1. How does your communication reveal a frustration with people and circumstances?
2. In what ways is your communication an attempt to take control?
3. How do you typically respond when your plans are thwarted?
4. How do you respond when God sends suffering or disappointment your way?
5. Do you encourage those around you to rest in God's sovereign care? Do you point to evidences of his loving hand? How?
6. Do you seek to speak in a way that encourages the work God is doing in others?
7. Do your words reveal that you are resting in God's control or wrestling with it?

Take time with these questions, and ask God to help you to be honest. Be sensitive to the convicting ministry of the Holy Spirit as you answer. Remember that God reveals our hearts not to discourage us but to draw us ever closer to the circle of his love. He corrects those he loves.

Chapter Six

Following the King for All the Wrong Reasons

Don't waste your energy striving for perishable food. . . .Work for the food that sticks with you, food that nourishes your lasting life, food the Son of Man provides. (John 6:27)

I sat with him in his living room, struck by the things he was saying. It was not that I hadn't heard this kind of thing before, but he spoke with such strength of feeling. It had come at the end of a day when Josh's two young children seemed to make an unending chorus of whining demands. His job seemed only to take more and more out of him, and he and his wife weren't exactly feeling appreciative of one another. He dropped his body down on the couch and stared for a while at the floor. You could almost see Josh steaming.

Then he said, "Why do I do it? What's it all worth? All the years of Bible study and prayer, all the times I've gone to church. . . . I struggle to do what is right, and what do I get? A life that is impossible! People say, 'Just trust the Lord.' For what? He doesn't answer, he doesn't care. I just blew it! I shouldn't have gotten married, I should never have had children, I can't handle this job, and God just sits up there and lets it all happen. So I'm a Christian! What good has it done me? I'm tired, I'm overwhelmed with my responsibilities, and

I see no way out. But if I leave all this, I get punished. What's wrong with this picture?"

I was not the only person to hear Josh talk this way. The same discontent spilled over into his daily communication with his wife and children, in a steady stream of complaints, irritation, impatience, accusation, and sometimes even threats.

I tried to gently respond, but Josh was angry and unwilling to hear me. He hadn't really been talking to me anyway. I just happened to be in the room. It was a moment of brutal honesty that I just happened to witness. Josh's angry words revealed a great deal about the true thoughts and desires of his heart. Underneath the neat-looking, everything's-fine-with-me exterior that people saw at Sunday worship was a man whose heart was at war with God. Josh had followed the King, and it hadn't turned out the way he had expected.

As we've noted from Luke 6, the words we speak come out of our hearts. This means that in some way our talk tends to reveal the true love(s) of our hearts. What was wrong with Josh's talk was not just the particular words he spoke or the particular tone he used. We wouldn't solve his communication problem by telling him never to say those words again. To see lasting change in Josh's speech, the doubt and discontent beneath his words needed to be exposed. We needed to deal with the true love(s) of Josh's heart. What was going on with Josh? How had his conversation become so displeasing to God and so destructive to the people around him? Why wasn't his speech all it is supposed to be—loving, kind, encouraging, and seasoned with grace?

The reality revealed by Josh's words is the focus of this chapter. It is an issue we all must face if our communication is ever going to be what God wants it to be. Be honest and ask yourself, Is there a little of Josh in me? I know there is in *me*! There have been times when I've wondered if it's worth it. During those times it is easy to grumble and complain your way through the day.

The reality of the Christian struggle Josh experienced is important—and common. It is simply this: *Many of us follow the*

King for all the wrong reasons. It is not enough to be excited with the King. We need to be so for the right reason.

Whose Dream? Which Bread?

If you had to write down your dream for your life, what would you write? What is your "if only," "if I could just have," "if God would just give me . . . then I would be happy"? Maybe a better way to ask the question is, What kind of Messiah do you want Jesus to be in your life? Keep your answer in mind as we look at one of the most familiar stories in all of Scripture, found in John 6.

In this story, Jesus takes a little boy's lunch and by means of his messianic power turns it into a meal for five thousand people with twelve baskets of food left over. Imagine your reaction if you had been there, and consider the impact of this man's power on your life. The crowd is buzzing, "This is it. This is the prophet, the Messiah. He's come. Let's grab him quickly and make him our king! This is what we've been waiting for all these years."

You would think that this is the golden moment for Jesus. Didn't he come to be this people's king? Isn't he the prophet of prophets? Of course he is. But notice what Jesus does. He leaves. He withdraws. He disappears. What is going on? Why does he respond so strangely? The crowd looks all over for Jesus. They want to make him their king, but he doesn't seem to want anything to do with it. Why? Isn't this just what he came for?

In John 6:25, Jesus has crossed the Sea of Galilee and the crowd finds him there.

> When they found him on the other side of the lake, they asked him, "Rabbi, when did you get here?"
>
> Jesus answered, "I tell you the truth, you are looking for me, not because you saw miraculous signs but because you ate the loaves and had your fill. Do not work for food that spoils,

but for food that endures to eternal life, which the Son of Man will give you. On him God the Father has placed his seal of approval."

Then they asked him, "What must we do to do the works God requires?"

Jesus answered, "The work of God is this: to believe in the one he has sent."

So they asked him, "What miraculous sign then will you give that we may see it and believe you? What will you do? Our forefathers ate the manna in the desert; as it is written: 'He gave them bread from heaven to eat.'"

Jesus said to them, "I tell you the truth, it is not Moses who has given you the bread from heaven, but it is my Father who gives you the true bread from heaven. For the bread of God is he who comes down from heaven and gives life to the world."

"Sir," they said, "from now on give us this bread."

Then Jesus declared, "I am the bread of life. He who comes to me will never go hungry, and he who believes in me will never be thirsty. But as I told you, you have seen me and still you do not believe." (vv. 25–36)

What is Jesus saying to these people about their desire to make him their king? Is he joyful, encouraged, ready to respond? No, instead of thanking them, he rebukes them. He essentially says, "You've missed the whole point."

In writing his Gospel, John does something very helpful. He doesn't like to call the miracles that Jesus performed *miracles*. He likes to call them *signs*. What does a sign do? It points to something else, the reality you really seek or the place you really want to be. For example, when you take a vacation, you don't stop at the road sign with your family and say, "We're here! We're here! Get the kids and unpack, honey." No, you follow the sign and drive on until you have reached your actual destination. The sign along the road only points to the reality.

This is what was wrong with these people and their reaction

to Christ. They had experienced the *miracle*, but they didn't see the *sign*. The physical blessing of bread was meant to point to a much deeper spiritual reality and, Christ said, "You're not getting it." They were concentrating on the miracle of the bread as if it were the ultimate reality. Christ is very pointed in what he says. The terminology he uses when he says, "You've had your bellies filled" could literally be translated, "You've grazed." He is saying, "You've grazed till you're full, but you still haven't gotten it."

What was behind these people's pursuit of Christ? What did they really want? I do not believe that they pursued Christ out of a humble submission to his messiahship and a willingness to follow him wherever he would lead. Their pursuit of Christ was born instead out of a love for self and the hope that Christ would be the one who would meet their felt needs. They were excited about following the King—but for all the wrong reasons.

I am afraid that many of us respond to Jesus in the same way. What moves and motivates everything we do is not a submission to God's will and a burning desire for his glory, but our own set of personal desires and dreams. We are excited about the King because we see him as the most efficient delivery system for those dreams. You can tell what really excites us when we fall into discouragement and grumbling, when he does not deliver the "good" that we want. The lips that once praised now complain, and the lips that once encouraged now accuse. To avoid this we must learn to ask, Whose dream are we really pursuing? Which bread do we really want? Here again this struggle of the heart will shape the communication of our lips.

Physical Bread and Spiritual Deception

This struggle of physical versus spiritual bread is a core struggle of the Christian life. It is a core struggle of *human* life.

In the middle of this struggle is the Deceiver, who would have us believe that life is all about physical bread, that spiritual things are of little consequence. We are bombarded with this message from birth. It is all around us in magazines, newspapers, TV, on billboards, in the mall, and in conversations on the subway or at work. Life is about how much physical bread you have been able to gain, maintain, and enjoy. True happiness is found, we are told, in people, possessions, and positions. And since we "only go around once," the beer ad tells us that we should do it with all the "gusto" we've got.

This struggle over bread is depicted in many biblical passages. It is at the heart of Satan's temptation of Christ (Matt. 4:1–11). It is tragically played out as Judas sells the Messiah for thirty pieces of silver (Matt. 26:14–15). It is a very potent form of the human tendency to exchange worship and service of the Creator for worship and service of the created thing (Rom. 1:21–25). It is what John warns against when he calls us to forsake the love of the world (1 John 2:13–15), and it is graphically portrayed in Christ's parable of the rich fool, who builds bigger barns to store his goods, only to die and meet his Maker (Luke 12:13–21). Paul discusses this struggle in terms of living with an eye on eternity, saying that he fixes his eyes "not on what is seen, but on what is unseen" (2 Cor. 4:16–18). Psalm 73 also reveals this struggle as the psalmist envies the affluence and ease of the wicked. The message of the Deceiver is all around us, making this a core spiritual struggle for every human being.

Embedded in the Deceiver's tempting message are four subtle lies. They seem to offer life, but accepting them leads to death. Each lie is meant to move us away from the very thing for which we were created, a life of love and submission to the Creator. Let's consider these four subtle but persuasive lies:

1. *Physical things are permanent.* The Bible tells us so many times in so many ways that the world is passing away. John says, "The world and its desires pass away" (1 John 2:17). Paul tells us that "outwardly we are wasting away" (2 Cor. 4:16). The

psalmist says that the lives of the wicked with their abundance are like a dream that quickly passes when one awakes (Ps. 73:18–20). And this is why Christ enjoins us to "provide purses for yourselves that will not wear out, a treasure in heaven that will not be exhausted, where no thief comes near and no moth destroys" (Luke 12:33).

2. *Physical bread is the only bread.* Sinners tend to deify the creation and elevate its significance over the One who made it. They tend to forsake the pursuit of the unseen God for the amassing of personal possessions. This is why we are encouraged not to store up treasures on earth but to seek first his kingdom (Matt. 6:19–34). And this is why we are told to live as pilgrims, as tent-dwellers, not giving ourselves over to the accumulation of material things as if they were the only bread that really counts. The person who believes this lie is a fool (Luke 12:20).

3. *Human success is defined by the amount of physical bread you possess.* Who among us has not envied the rich? Which of us has not dreamed of winning the lottery and living the idyllic life that would follow? Who hasn't thought at some moment that we would be happier if we only had more money? Who of us isn't a little moved by the images of money, power, and success that are beamed at us on TV? Who among us doesn't want to peek through the gates to see how the "other half" lives?

Scripture aims these powerful words to us at such moments: "What good will it be for a man if he gains the whole world, yet forfeits his soul? Or what can a man give in exchange for his soul?" (Matt. 16:26). Christ speaks directly to this lie, saying, "Watch out! Be on your guard against all kinds of greed; a man's life does not consist in the abundance of his possessions" (Luke 12:15). Jesus defined human success in terms of two fundamental commitments: to love God above all else and to love your neighbor as yourself (Matt. 22:37–40). To live this way is to be rich no matter how small your collection of worldly things.

4. *Life is found in physical bread.* This is the lie of lies—that somehow, some way, life can be found outside of a relationship with God. This was the lie told by the Deceiver in the Garden, and it is the lie told countless times again every day. Feeding on physical bread only leads to more hunger. It is only as you feed on Christ by faith, receiving his life, that you can ever be satisfied. He is *the* Bread. He *is* life! All other offers of life outside of Christ lead parched people to drink at dry wells. He is the True Bread. He is the river of life. Follow him and within you will flow rivers of living water (John 4:13–14). Without him you are dead, even though you physically live (Eph. 2:1–10).

It is so easy to buy into the lie that life can be found in human acceptance, possessions, and position. It is so easy to have your life controlled by dreams of success in your career. It is so easy to believe that nothing satisfies like romantic love. It is so easy to fall into pursuing the idol images of Western culture— big suburban house, luxurious car, lavish vacations, etc. When we do this, we quit feeding on Christ. Our devotional life begins to suffer. We pray less, and when we do, we pray more selfishly. We find our schedule doesn't leave much time for ministry, and we spend more time with our colleagues at work than we do with brothers and sisters in the body of Christ. Functionally, we are feeding on the world's bread, not on Christ.

Our entire life will be determined by which bread we pursue. There are no more dangerous lies than the ones that lead us away from a loving hope and surrender to the Creator we cannot see, and toward a bondage to an endless, unsatisfying pursuit of what is passing away.

Whose Dream—Christ's or Yours?

Now consider your own life: your marriage, job, children, friends, home, and church. What do you want of Christ?

Whose dream do you bring before him? Is your dream nothing more than your personal definition of paradise? I'm sure every husband and wife has dreamed of the perfect mate. Every parent has dreamed of the perfect child. Every child has dreamed of the perfect mom and dad. Every worker has dreamed of the perfect boss. Every one of us has dreamed of the perfect friend or the perfect church with the perfect pastor. Each of us has dreamed of the perfect house and the perfect financial life where every bill is easily paid. But the question here is this: What is the deepest level of your hunger today? Do you find yourself discontent with the present? Do you struggle with what God has given you today? Peter says important things about what *now* is all about.

> *Praise be to the God and Father of our Lord Jesus Christ! In his great mercy he has given us new birth into a living hope through the resurrection of Jesus Christ from the dead, and into an inheritance that can never perish, spoil or fade—kept in heaven for you, who through faith are shielded by God's power until the coming of the salvation that is ready to be revealed in the last time. (1 Peter 1:3–5)*

This sounds wonderful, doesn't it? Peter says, "Don't you understand what you have? You have been saved by God's mercy. Your sins have been forgiven. You are part of God's family. And not only that, but there's an inheritance waiting for you that won't spoil, won't perish, and won't fade."

"Yes," we respond, "this is wonderful!"

But we need to read on. Peter has been talking about the past, and our forgiveness by God's mercy. And he has been talking about the future, and our coming inheritance. But what about now? What is going on in the present? Let's pick up where we left off.

> *. . . who through faith are shielded by God's power until the coming of the salvation that is ready to be revealed in the last*

*time. In this you greatly rejoice, though now for a little while
you have had to suffer grief in all kinds of trials. These have
come so that your faith—of greater worth than gold, which
perishes even though refined by fire—may be proved genuine
and may result in praise, glory and honor when Jesus Christ
is revealed. Though you have not seen him, you love him;
and even though you do not see him now, you believe in him
and are filled with an inexpressible and glorious joy, for you
are receiving the goal of your faith, the salvation of your
souls. (vv. 5–9)*

What is *now* about? Living in the present is about something much deeper than getting up in the morning with a
smile, much more than a satisfying job, romantic weekends
with your wife, encouraging friendships, well-mannered children, a nice house in a good community. It's more than a pastor who really seems to care about you, and more than a bud-
get that seems to be working.

Peter's point is that God is willing to compromise things
like these to produce something greater, fuller, and deeper in
us: genuine faith. This is what God is after in the experiences
that make us wonder if he really loves us, if he hears our
prayers, experiences that cause us to envy other believers, or
maybe even people who don't know him. Why are those experiences sent our way? Because God is not done with us yet.
He is at work giving us the goal of our faith, the salvation of
our souls. Rather than grumbling and complaining and
doubting the faithfulness of God, we should be able to respond with worship. Instead of "God, why me?" we should be
able to say, "God, thank you. I want more of your salvation.
Lord, I want all that you can give me. I know you are not done
with me yet." The struggles are not a mistake. They are tokens
of redemptive love. Trials should not lead us to *doubt* the love
of the King; they should *convince* us of it.

In my opinion, in the heart of every sinner is a desire that
life would be a resort. You pay your money and you get what-

ever you want, whenever you want it. Someone explained one of these offers to me. He said, "Twelve stated meals a day." Twelve! Then he said, "The last meal is at midnight, and at 2:00 A.M. you can order pizza in your room if you want it." Sounds like fun to me! No one can say no to you! At any moment you can decide to do whatever you want. If God wanted life to be a resort, this is what it would be like.

Recognizing the Signs

Now catch the principle here. The blessings God gives you in your family, job, home, church, friends, and community are meant to do something for you. They are meant to point you to the deeper and fuller blessing of the presence of the Lord Jesus Christ in your life. He *is* life! Abundant life is not your spouse, children, house, car, possessions, job, friends, or church. Abundant life is Jesus Christ! The amazing reality is that he is ours and we are his! This is the bread worth living for. Not the bread of physical blessing, but the spiritual bread, Christ, that his gift of earthly bread represents. Some of us are only excited about Christ because we think he will deliver more physical bread. We fall into spiritual depression when he removes the physical bread so that we would hunger again for the Bread that really satisfies. Can you see beyond the physical bread to see Christ and the glories of his grace? Or do you consume the physical bread without any desire for the spiritual blessings that he gives: love, joy, peace, patience, kindness, goodness, faithfulness, gentleness, and self-control?

In John 6, Jesus says, "I am the bread of life." Ask yourself this question: Which bread do I hunger for? What kind of bread do I really want to feed on? I'm not saying that physical things are of no consequence or that we should not seek to improve our lives (marriages, jobs, churches, families, etc.), but I think that we can miss the point. We too can see the miracles and miss the sign. We can rejoice over jobs given, friendships restored, homes supplied, and bills paid and fail to hunger for the spiritual blessings that physical provisions represent. We can be like the people who pursued Jesus only to keep their stomachs full. They didn't really want him as their King. They wanted him to be their Great Waiter, dedicated to keeping them physically satisfied.

Many of us come to Jesus today because we are holding onto our dream and we want Jesus to somehow help us get it. If we are honest, we would have to admit that this is all we really want from him. And if we don't get it, we are miserably disappointed.

If we are living for earthly bread and see it as our source of life, we are going to be in big trouble when we don't have it. But if we are living for spiritual bread, for a deeper communion with Jesus Christ, then our lives (with all of their problems) become wonderful places to know and grow in fellowship with the One who *is* life. We will live out this pursuit of the true Bread in the bedrooms, kitchens, job sites, neighborhoods, and hallways of life. And this will have implications for our communication.

When you have a community of people (family, friends, body of Christ) who are committed to Christ, long to know him better, and want their lives to express praise, worship, and glory to him, their talk will be affected. Their words will encourage and strengthen, and they will experience unity and an intimacy of fellowship that the world doesn't know. When we let go of our personal dreams and expectations, we can experience the unity of the Spirit we have been given as the children of God.

In contrast, people whose eyes are focused on physical bread will eat one another up. Their talk will be the world of trouble described in James 3, because this bread cannot satisfy. Love for it will cause you to be a parasite on those around you, sucking the blood from them, though they can never, ever, ever, ever give you enough. There's only one Bread—it's Jesus. Life is found in feeding on him by faith. There is no other way.

Disillusioned Disciples

Do you remember what happened when Jesus proclaimed that message? Jesus said to the crowd, "Unless you eat the flesh of the Son of Man and drink his blood, you have no life in you" (John 6:53). Not only did the crowd forsake him, but many of his disciples left as well (v. 66). They said, "This is a hard teaching" (v. 60). They were right. The hard call of the gospel is that God sent his Son not so that we could realize our agenda, but that we could be part of his.

I encourage you, as a reader, to start here with humble honesty. What does your talk reveal of the true love(s) of your heart? What is the deep inner hunger that you live to satisfy? Is it hunger for Christ? If he is what your heart craves, there are wonderful opportunities to grow in grace and knowledge in the midst of all kinds of difficulty. These experiences, Peter reminds us, are sent our way by a God who remembers us with redemptive love. He is completing the saving work he has begun in us. We will be refined by trial. Life is not a resort, but a bumpy pathway that leads to conformity to Christ. We can face the bumps with genuine joy, knowing that every bump was placed in our path by a loving heavenly Father for our redemptive good.

I once was talking with a lady who had been married for many years. She was married to a person who, very honestly, I would have to say was a bad man. He was angry, controlling, and manipulative. He regularly said and did hurtful things. She, meanwhile, had dreamed of the ultimate husband and had gotten so embittered by the blessing of other women in her church that she said she could no longer go to worship. She felt as if God had forsaken her, so much so that she couldn't read her Bible or pray.

I wanted her to understand her identity in Christ and the love of the Lord. I wanted her to understand that God is a refuge and strength, an ever-present help in trouble, so I quoted a few passages to her that spoke of God's amazing love when, in the middle of a verse, she said, "Stop!" I looked up at her angry face. She said, "Don't tell me any more that God loves me. I want a *husband* who loves me!" And she pounded her fist on her chair as she spoke.

I learned something that day. To the degree that you have based your life on something other than the Lord, to that degree God's love and the hope of the gospel will not comfort you. You will not be comforted because you are hungry for another kind of bread. You long for a king who will give you the bread you crave. That bread might be a relationship, circumstance, or position. It might be human love and respect, the desire for vengeance, or a certain economic state. It literally can be anything in creation! But there are only two types of bread: Christ, the Living Bread, and everything else. We set our hearts either on him or on something else.

I learned something else that day. That angry lady's words revealed the true love of her heart, her dream, the bread her heart craved. Certainly, she would have said that she was a believer; she would have professed faith in the truths of Scripture. She probably even would have said that she loved the Lord. However, her prayers were not an expression of thanks, but a list of demands in the form of requests. Her words that day revealed that despite her profession of faith, she really sought a king who would do her bidding. She expected God to deliver her dream and she was angry that he hadn't. She had no eyes to see that through the vehicle of a difficult marriage, her King desired to give her something better. As we look at our own lives and all that we are living for, we need to ask, Whose dream, which bread do we seek?

The question before us is this: What happens to us when we don't get the dream? Do we wallow in self-pity? Do we lash out, blaming those around us? Do we get swallowed up in envy and covetousness? Do we begin verbalizing doubt of the goodness, faithfulness, and love of God? Do we find it hard to worship, praise, read the Bible, pray, fellowship with other believers, or share the gospel with those who don't know the Lord?

What do our words tell us? Do they tell us that we are living for earthly bread? God's goodness, love, power, glory, and call to us do not change in the absence of earthly bread. If *he* is the object of our hunger, we can have joy even in the middle of suffering. Whose bread are we really seeking? What is revealed by our reactions and words? Perhaps many of us, even though we have not physically forsaken the King, have lost our enthusiasm for his grace and mercy because following him has not led to the fulfillment of our dreams. In our hearts, we too have left him, like the disciples who walked sadly away when he called them to a commitment of faith.

What Happens When the Dream Is Gone?

An Old Testament prophet (Habakkuk) looked around at the people of God and said, "God, I don't understand what is going on here. You've stood by and allowed your people to be very wicked. Why do you permit this? Why don't you do something about the sin of your people?" God responded, "I *will* do something. I will send an evil, violent nation from the north to come down and wipe my people out."

The prophet could not believe what he was hearing! When he asked God to do something, he had been thinking revival—judgment was not in his catalog! He protested, "God, how can you do this? How can you use a nation more evil than we are to judge us? It doesn't make any sense!" The prophet debated with God and, in the middle of the debate, God revealed his power and glory to him. Habakkuk ends his book with these precious words:

> *Though the fig tree does not bud*
> *and there are no grapes on the vines,*
> *though the olive crop fails*

and the fields produce no food,
   though there are no sheep in the pen
   and no cattle in the stalls,
yet I will rejoice in the LORD,
   I will be joyful in God my Savior.
The Sovereign LORD is my strength;
   he makes my feet like the feet of a deer,
   he enables me to go on the heights. (Hab. 3:17–19)

The prophet has described the total decimation of a farming culture. There is nothing left—no plants, trees, or animals. There is no physical bread. In the face of this, Habakkuk says, "Lord, though everything is gone, yet I will rejoice because you, my Savior and my Lord, my Life and my Strength, are still here!"

If your dream would crumble, if there were nothing left, would you rise in the midst of your tears and say, "I am full of joy, because the Lord is my lord, the Lord is my life, the Lord is my strength, and gloriously, in the midst of all this loss and destruction, I have him"? You can pursue your dream, or you can pursue the Lord's dream for you. You can ask him to conform you to his image, so that more and more your life and your words would bring him praise. Or you can wish that Christ would conform to the scope and focus of *your* dream. Whose dream are you seeking?

May God help us to be people who see the sign behind the miracle, who look at earthly blessing and say, "These blessings point me to the deeper, fuller reality of Christ in my life. What I hunger for and what I want my life to be about is fellowship with, love for, and obedience to my Lord Jesus Christ." My prayer is that both you and I would be people who follow Jesus even when there are no more harvests, no more animals, and no more bread. My prayer is that we would be people who rise up in the morning and say, "I am filled with joy! I am a child of the King. He is my life and I will follow him by faith."

Your Dreams and Your Talk

As you might expect, the truths of John 6 have important ramifications for the way we think about communication. John 6 points us to the core issue of our words: Our words are shaped by the dream that resides in our hearts. They are determined by the bread we are seeking.

Take a husband and wife, for example. If each is holding on tightly to a personal dream, feeding on earthly bread, they will inevitably experience frustration and disappointment with each other and much conflict as their dreams collide. Their world of talk will surely be a world of trouble. They will find themselves cursing the spouse God gave them and at times may even utter resentful curses at God. Their tongues will only be tamed when their hearts are controlled by the rule of the King, the dream of the King, and the bread of the King.

As sinners we have a tendency to be excited about following the King for all the wrong reasons. This infects our words with the poison of selfishness and saps the life out of our praise to the Lord and our ministry to others. We no longer find joy in being his disciples, and we too will walk sadly away. When our words reveal that we have left a position of hope, trust, and rest in the King to feed on bread that can never, ever satisfy, we need to return to him and pray,

Lord, it is so easy to get caught up in our own desires and dreams. It's so easy to think of you as little more than the deliverer of those dreams. Too often we get excited like the multitude and lose sight of the spiritual reality behind the gifts you give us.

Lord, we pray that we would not just pursue our own hopes and dreams, but have a hunger and thirst for Jesus Christ, and a desire to know his will in every area of our lives. May we stand before you in love and joyful submission, feeding on you by faith. May we be strong in joy, faith, courage, and obedience even when we aren't experiencing physical bread. In the midst of trials may we say to you and of you, "Thank you, Lord, for your love. Thank you that you are busy completing your saving work in us." For this we need your help and we pray that all of this would be for your glory. Amen.

Getting Personal:
Getting to the Heart of Your Talk

How can we tell what is really ruling our hearts? Ask yourself these questions:

1. What happens to my prayers and my talk about God when I don't get what I want?
2. How do I speak to others when they seem to stand in the way of my dream?
3. What happens to my talk when circumstances are difficult and unpleasant?
4. What happens to my talk when I see others blessed while I struggle?
5. How much do my prayers focus on the deeper heart changes that God is working within me and the wider concerns of his kingdom work?
6. How much does my talk express a spirit of thankfulness and contentment?
7. Do my words encourage others to put their trust and rest in the Lord?
8. How often is grumbling and complaining a regular part of my everyday conversation?
9. Does my speech evidence gentleness, kindness, and patience?
10. Is my communication infected with demanding, critical, impatient, accusatory, or condemning words?
11. What happens to my talk when others sin against me?

12. What happens when my prayers are not answered as I would expect?
13. As I seek to humbly answer these questions, what dreams of my heart are revealed? What do I do with them?

Chapter Seven

Speaking for the King

God authorized and commanded me to commission you: Go out and train everyone you meet. . . . (Matt. 28:18)

WE live in the age of the omnipresent video. It's as if our lives are being lived on tape. Families videotape their holidays, birthday parties, vacations, and humorous pratfalls. They even hide a video camera in the family room to tape the babysitter and ensure that she is not abusing the children. There are security cameras at the convenience store, the supermarket, and the bank. Nothing of any note takes place in our communities—be it a celebration, parade, police chase, election, accident, fire, or natural disaster—without the video camera present to record the moment.

One day I was standing on a pier, watching someone videotape fish, when this question hit me: If someone were to watch the videotape of my life, what would they conclude about me? What would they say I am living for? What would they say is my mission in life?

My mind went further. How would they view my interactions with people? What, for example, would they say about the way I treat my family? What would they make of my marriage, my parenting, and my relationship to neighbors? What would they conclude I was living for?

As a counselor, I often find that when someone is telling me his story, he often does a much better job describing the actions, reactions, and words of others than he does his own. And I often find myself saying, "You know, we've been watching the videotape of your life, but there's something curious about it: *You're not in it!* It has all the important people in your life, with their reactions and words, but not you. Let's turn the camera to see how you are dealing with all that is going on in your life. Let's see what's important to you and how you deal with the situations and relationships you encounter every day."

I would like to do the same thing with you as a reader. Let me encourage you to focus particularly on your conversational life. If I watched a videotape of your life, paying special attention to your communication with the important people in your world, what would I find? What would I think you are seeking to accomplish? What would I conclude was important to you?

This chapter is about God's *mission* for our mouths. We started this book by saying that our words belong to the Lord. They were created by him, exist through him, and are to be used for him. We were given the ability to communicate so that our words would help us do his work and bring him glory. He is the source, the standard, and the goal of all our talk. He is the Lord of our mouths! So, it is vital that we have a clear sense of his purposes for us in this area. Once we do, we need to review our videotapes and ask, Are we speaking for the King?

When we talk about God's mission for our mouths, we are talking about a responsibility we have been given to carry out. A mission is a particular set of objectives that gives order and purpose to what a person or group does. It is a special assignment, an inner calling, to pursue a particular activity. Our question is, What mission does the Great Speaker have for our mouths? We need a clear answer to this question before we look at all the practical Scripture passages on communication.

We also need to see how the Great Deceiver seeks to tempt us away from God's goal for our talk.

No passage more clearly and succinctly defines God's mission for our talk than 2 Corinthians 5:11–21.

Since, then, we know what it is to fear the Lord, we try to persuade men. What we are is plain to God, and I hope it is also plain to your conscience. We are not trying to commend ourselves to you again, but are giving you an opportunity to take pride in us, so that you can answer those who take pride in what is seen rather than what is in the heart. If we are out of our mind, it is for the sake of God; if we are in our right mind, it is for you. For Christ's love compels us, because we are convinced that one died for all, and therefore all died. And he died for all, that those who live should no longer live for themselves but for him who died for them and was raised again.

So from now on we regard no one from a worldly point of view. Though we once regarded Christ in this way, we do so no longer. Therefore, if anyone is in Christ, he is a new creation; the old has gone, the new has come! All this is from God, who reconciled us to himself through Christ and gave us the ministry of reconciliation; that God was reconciling the world to himself in Christ, not counting men's sin against them. And he has committed to us the message of reconciliation. We are therefore Christ's ambassadors, as though God were making his appeal through us. We implore you on Christ's behalf: Be reconciled to God. God made him who had no sin to be sin for us, so that in him we might become the righteousness of God.

Called to Be Ambassadors

One Thursday night I went to my son's room to say hello and to discuss some arrangements that needed to be made for the weekend. I knocked on his door, walked into his room, and encountered a scene of total destruction! I don't know how he found his clothes (I think all of them were on the floor at the time) or how he found his bed to sleep (a corner of it stuck out from under the rubble). There were college textbooks, shoes, magazines, music equipment, CDs, skateboard parts, and a host of other unrecognizable objects. My anger and frustration were immediate. I remember thinking, *He is sitting here in the middle of this mess and it doesn't bother him at all!*

He greeted me rather warmly and I let it fly! I forgot all about saying hello or asking him about his day. Instead I went into a tirade on the condition of his room and how I was sure that it mirrored the condition of his life (which was actually not true). I angrily reminded him of how hard I work to provide him with the things that were strewn everywhere. I asked him what it would be like if his mother and I kept the whole house that way. I lectured on and asked questions—questions I didn't give him any time to answer because they weren't really questions. I was just venting. I told him I didn't know how he could stand being in that room the way it was, but I knew I couldn't. I told him that it better be cleaned up quickly and I left.

I walked down the hallway feeling angry and empty and threw myself down on the family room couch. It hit me then that I hadn't discussed *anything* I had intended to discuss. I did my best to justify my behavior: (1) The room was a mess (very true). (2) It did evidence poor stewardship on his part (true). (3) He did need someone to confront him with this issue (also true). But with all of this, I knew that what I had done was wrong. This encounter would not produce positive changes in my son, and I knew that God was not well pleased. I prayed for forgiveness, got myself together, and went back in to talk to my son the right way.

Paul's words in 2 Corinthians 5 explain in detail what was wrong with my "conversation" that night. If we are ever going to speak up to God's standard and according to his design, we need to understand the practical principles that flow out of this passage.

1. *We need to speak with an understanding that we are God's ambassadors.* A political ambassador is someone who has been called from his or her homeland to live in another and represent the message, methods, and character of his leader (president, king, prime minister, etc.). Paul's message here is radical and dramatic: we have been called to be ambassadors of *the* King! God has put us just where he wants us *to represent him*. If I am ever going to speak as he has ordained for me to speak, I must be aware of my ambassador status. I am where I am because I am called to represent the Lord. Paul says that for the Christian, the old life that was structured around self-interest is gone. We are new creations; the old has passed away. Dead and gone is the life in which we only served our own interests and did just about anything to get what we wanted. No, Paul says we have been reconciled to God and this has given us a new ministry—his work of reconciliation.

We are not free to advance our own interests with our talk. Our communication must always have an ambassadorial agenda (the mission, methods, and character of the King). But we need to be honest here. There is no situation in life without a struggle between our own interests and the Lord's. There are always things we want in certain ways and at certain times. It is always easy to move away from God's purposes toward our own. The shifts between the two can be subtle and deceptive, especially since as believers we are still not free from the sin of self-interest. It remains one of the fundamental heart sins that lie beneath our words. This tendency toward self-interest is what the position of ambassador so pointedly addresses. You *cannot* be a successful ambassador if you are primarily motivated by your own interests! You cannot be an ambassador part-time. You must always remember that you are where you are because you are a representative. *You have been sent by the King to speak for him.*

There is another way to think about this ambassadorial calling. We have been called to represent the King in a way that *incarnates* him. To incarnate means to embody in human form, to personify. This is a position of majestic honor given to unworthy sinners. If we could understand the wonder of it all, we would be amazed that we could do or say *anything* that could picture God's glory! But this is just what God has chosen us to do: to embody his mission, methods, and character on earth. We are his hands, his eyes, his ears, and his mouths. We put flesh and blood to who he is and what he wants for those around us. We are called to make his character and will seen, heard, and known. This was my job description the night I went into my son's room, but I had lost all sense of my calling. I was there full of my own interest, and there was no incarnational agenda to my words at all.

When we live and speak incarnationally, we mirror the work Christ did on earth: he came to make the Father known. While he was here, Jesus said that the works he did and the words he spoke were not his own, but came from his Father (see John 14:5–14). Jesus was committed to the Father's will in the things he did and said because he understood that his mission was incarnational. He had taken on flesh for the purpose of making God known. Now, in the same way that Christ revealed the Father, we are called to reveal Christ. We are called to incarnate Jesus, the Reconciler and Redeemer. This is why our words always have an agenda higher than our own purposes or desires.

I love the way Paul talks about this higher, incarnational agenda. He says that it's "as though God were making his appeal through us" (2 Cor. 5:20). To speak as an ambassador means that we are always asking what God wants to accomplish in our hearts and in our listeners' hearts. What appeal is he making? The three words I have been using are helpful here: *mission, methods,* and *character.*

Speaking as an ambassador means speaking in a way that represents the *mission* (that is, the will and purposes) of the

King. It means asking, Do my words capture what is valuable to the Lord? It also means considering the *methods* of the King. This means asking, How would the Lord respond to this person in this situation? Here we look to the Lord as our ultimate model of behavior. Our calling is to respond as he responded, to act as he acted, and to speak as he spoke. Finally, speaking as an ambassador requires thinking about the *character* of the King. Representing the Lord is not only a matter of right goals and right methods, but right attitude as well. Here we ask, As I respond to this person in this situation, am I faithfully representing the character of the King (see Col. 3:12–14)? If I had asked myself these questions that night in my son's room, it would have dramatically altered my words.

The Mission of the King

2. *Ambassadors need to speak out of a clear understanding of the King's mission.* What is he doing on earth? In our lives? In this situation at this moment? What is his mission? Again, Paul lays this out very clearly for us. He tells us that God is working so that "those who live should no longer live for themselves but for him who died for them and was raised again" (2 Cor. 5:15). God's focus is on our hearts and our tendency toward idolatry. As we saw earlier, the most powerful and pervasive of all idols is the idol of self. All sinners serve it in some way. Like Adam and Eve, every sinner has the desire to be God and to have the world operate according to his or her pleasure and will. Jesus lived, died, and was raised again to break our bondage to this idol. His goal for us is that we who once lived for ourselves would be turned, by his grace, to worship and serve him alone. As he changes us, more and more we will be like him. We will be able to truly represent him, and as his ambassadors, we will be able to speak in ways that contribute to his purposes in others' lives as well as our own.

Notice that the target of our mission is the heart, the seat of worship, either of God or of idols. As God's ambassadors, we must speak with the heart in focus. This does not come naturally to human beings. Most of the time, we talk about the physical stuff of life—jobs, homes, cars, people, and possessions. Our words reflect our attempt to get what we want or our frustrations when we fail. A husband yells at his wife when she is taking too long getting ready. A mom yells at her daughter over her messy room, or a son complains that his clothes make him look like a "geek." A toddler throws a fit when he does not get to visit his favorite toy store, or a father blows up because he can't find his newspaper.

All of this communication focuses on the physical world and flows out of hearts that worship and serve the creation more than the Creator. It subtly deifies the creation and forgets the Creator's will and glory. Because this talk is itself idolatrous, God will never use it to accomplish his mission, which is freeing people from their bondage to all kinds of idols.

God's agenda in these moments is fundamentally spiritual. He knows that only when he owns our hearts unchallenged will we relate to the world in the way he has ordained. For this reason, God is focused not only on the momentary solution to our problems but on a long-term change of heart. He wants to recapture the hearts of his people so that they will serve him alone (see Ezek. 14:1–6). To accomplish this, he is willing to sacrifice our personal comfort. He will permit situations to "push our buttons," as my son's messy room pushed mine. He wants our heart sins to be revealed because we need to see them in order to repent! Very often, our hearts are most clearly revealed by our words. When our words do more harm than good, most likely we are speaking at cross-purposes with the King. Most likely, we are serving our own self-interest rather than his redemptive agenda. This is what God is concerned about most of all.

That night in my son's room, I had completely lost my awareness of the war that was raging for my son's heart. I didn't see him as an immortal soul. I didn't see him as a creature of

God who was in the midst of a spiritual battle. I forgot that my own struggle was not with flesh and blood, but with principalities and powers (Eph. 6:12). I forgot who both of us were in God's eyes. Instead, I got taken up with the creation (my son's room) and how I wanted it to be treated. Yes, I was on a mission—and unfortunately I was able to communicate my mission quite clearly! But I had forgotten that God had me there as an ambassador to represent *his* mission. In that I failed, and I missed a wonderful opportunity to be part of something higher, better, and more wonderful. I opted for physical bread and forgot the glory of the bread of life. Did the condition of that room reveal issues that needed attention? Yes, but only in a way that would represent the glorious bondage-breaking mission of the King.

The Method of the King

3. *Ambassadors need to speak with an understanding of the King's methods.* An ambassador is called not only to say *what* the King would say, but to say it in the *way* he would say it. We are not free to accomplish God's mission any way we see fit. The *way* we do what we are called to do must be consistent with his character and purposes. Again, this is part of being incarnational: our method of speaking should reflect the way God deals with his people.

Let's go back to that evening in my son's room. I was not only wrong in the goals I was pursuing, I was wrong in my methodology as well. How was I seeking to produce change? Through anger, guilt, condemnation, threat, and ultimatum. These were my "tools." But the One I am called to represent would not use these tools; they do not produce the long-term change of heart that is supposed to be my goal. Proverbs says that harsh words stir up anger (Prov. 15:1). They escalate hostility and defensiveness rather than produce the atmosphere of receptivity and openness that a gentle answer can produce.

How does God produce long-term heart change in us? Or, as Paul says it, how does he "compel" us away from living for ourselves to living for him? Second Corinthians 5:11–21 clearly teaches that the thing that compels Paul—and us—is the *love of Christ*. Ultimately, the thing that turns us is not just God's sovereignty, his holiness, his anger against sin, or his mighty power. It is the *kindness* of the Lord that leads people to repentance, we know from Romans 2:4. Paul says the same thing to the Corinthians—it is the love of Christ that draws us away from self and motivates us to live for him. Christ's glorious, substitutionary love is his most compelling argument for change—and his most powerful means of accomplishing it.

Think about this for a moment. In every setting and circumstance of life, we have been called to speak in a way that pictures the love of God. What a high and humbling standard! Who of us can say, "Yes, Lord, I am doing this"? Who among us does not need to honestly cry out and say, "Lord, I fall so far short of your calling. Come and be my strength or I will never speak in a way that makes your glory and goodness known"?

We need to humbly admit that the methods the Lord uses—and calls *us* to use—are very different from those we would naturally select. It is not my natural first response to bless the person who mistreats me (Rom. 12:14). It is not my tendency to forgive the person who is confessing the same sin for the seventh time that day (Luke 17:3–4). It is not my first choice to fight evil with good (Rom. 12:21) or to forsake revenge for peacemaking (vv. 17–20). I find it hard to be patient, gentle, humble, and persevering under provocation (Eph. 4:2). I would rather wait for the person who has offended me to come to me instead of going to him (Matt. 18:15–17). I find it difficult to settle issues and restore relationships before the sun sets; I want to hang on to offenses, and to replay the offense over and over again in my head (Eph. 4:26–27). I want to move people by the force of my hurt and anger, rather than by patient, humble forgiveness (James

1:20). I speak too quickly and find it tiresome to listen patiently and attentively (v. 19). I get caught up in the heat of the moment, instead of stepping back and preparing myself to speak in a godly way (Prov. 15:28).

But God doesn't think as we think. He doesn't do what we would naturally do, which is why we need to understand and follow his method. As Paul says in 2 Corinthians 10:4, "The weapons we fight with are not the weapons of the world. On the contrary, they have divine power to demolish strongholds." As ambassadors we are called to lay down the world's ineffective, even destructive, weapons and take up the gospel tools that the King has put in our hands. He will use them to bring radical heart change into our own lives and allow us to share in that same work with others.

Paul points to three tools (methods) of change in 2 Corinthians 5: *self-sacrifice, forgiveness,* and *reconciliation.* It's helpful to think of these terms not only as methods, but as boundaries for our words as his ambassadors. We cannot allow ourselves to speak words beyond these boundaries. Let's take a moment and consider what this would mean.

First, it is clear that the work Christ did in our lives required *self-sacrifice.* Our salvation meant his death. It is also clear from Scripture that he has called us, as his followers, to die to ourselves in order to serve and love others as he has loved us. The call to die to self, the call to purposeful self-sacrifice as his servants, was a consistent theme that the Lord taught his disciples during his time on earth (see Matt. 10:37–38; 16:24–28; Luke 9:23–27; 14:25–27, 31–33; John 12:23–26).

Christ changed us through his own self-sacrifice. We have become partakers of his divine nature because he was willing to lay down his life for us! If Christ had held onto his rights and authority as the Son of God, we would be hopelessly trapped in the bondage of sin, irrevocably destined for damnation. But Jesus was not only willing to leave the glory of heaven to suffer as a man on this broken, fallen earth; he was also willing to die for sins he had not committed! It is to this willingness for self-sacrifice that he calls us as his ambassadors, so that our lives might encourage his glorious work of change in people's hearts. Paul spoke of this to the church in Philippi.

If you have any encouragement from being united with Christ, if any comfort from his love, if any fellowship with the Spirit, if any tenderness and compassion, then make my joy complete by being like-minded, having the same love, being one in spirit and purpose. Do nothing out of selfish ambition or vain conceit, but in humility consider others better than yourselves. Each of you should look not only to your own interests, but also to the interests of others.

Your attitude should be the same as that of Christ Jesus:

Who, being in very nature God,
    did not consider equality with God something to be
        grasped,
but made himself nothing,
    taking on the very nature of a servant,
    being made in human likeness.
And being found in appearance as a man,
    he humbled himself
    and became obedient to death—
        even death on a cross! (Phil. 2:1–8)

Paul could not be more forceful about this call to follow Christ's example of self-sacrificing love. He says, "Do nothing out of selfish ambition or vain conceit." Our everyday talk must live up to this standard! Personally, I find it easy to be motivated by my personal rights and position. I struggle when I am asked to give up my time, my plans, my schedule, my possessions, and my control. Most of the trouble I get into with my talk occurs when I am trying to hold onto these things. I will speak impatiently to the daughter who has the audacity to be in the bathroom when I need to be in there. I will get irritated with my wife when her plans conflict with my schedule. I will lash out at the child who has inadvertently broken the knob on the stereo, or I will be tempted to pout when the family doesn't think my plan for the day is exciting and wonderful. What is wrong with all of these reactions? They are rooted in self-interest, so the communication that follows will *not* give glory to God or contribute to the work he is doing in my family.

The issue of self-sacrifice goes right to the core of my struggle as a sinner. Remember, the most powerful idol of all is the idol of self. The desire to be God resides in the heart of every sinner. This is *the* thing that God seeks to break in each of us so that we can live for his glory and not our own. As his ambassadors we are also called to die to self so that we may *speak* for him.

God's second tool (method) is *forgiveness*. It is amazing to consider that for reasons that only can be explained by his majestic love, Christ has fully and completely forgiven us! Paul says that God does not count men's sins against them. If our King, our Judge, the One who is completely holy is willing to forgive *us*, how can we do anything less for others? (See the powerful parable of the unmerciful servant in Matt. 18:21–35.) It is because of God's promise to fully and completely forgive us that we have come out of hiding, out of a life of excuses, blame-shifting, defensiveness, self-righteousness, and self-protection, to confess our sins. His forgiveness has been a powerful tool of change in our lives, and it will be a powerful tool of change as we represent him to others.

Sadly, the words I spoke to my son that evening were not spoken out of a forgiving heart. I had forgotten that I had been forgiven of much, much greater sins than the messiness of a room. I had forgotten the wonder of God's love and patient grace for me. I had no compassion for the chaotic life of a teenager. There was no slowness to speak and quickness to listen that should have characterized me as someone aware of his own sin and his own need for forgiveness. I asked no questions to stimulate my son to search his heart. I did not wait patiently for his answers. I offered no words of encouragement. Instead, I spoke out of a self-righteous heart that had forgotten that I needed God's grace as much as my son did. The two of us were not essentially different at that moment. We were and are the same—sinners in need of the forgiveness of God that brings radical change to our hearts. How could I forget the forgiveness I had been given? How could I not offer my son the same? God calls us to love as he has loved (John 13:34–35) and to forgive as he has forgiven us (Eph. 4:32–5:2). Our words must reach up, by the power of his Spirit, to this standard.

The third tool (method) the King uses to work change in us is *reconciliation*. To reconcile means to settle or resolve issues in order to restore a relationship. It is the work God does to restore our fellowship with him, the fellowship that was broken by sin. You can see this brokenness immediately after Adam and Eve ate the forbidden fruit. God came down to walk with them in the cool of the Garden, and he was confronted with something that had never happened before. Adam and Eve were hiding from him! Sin had broken their fellowship. Adam and Eve were now afraid of the God with whom they had enjoyed perfect communion. They sought to avoid him, and sinners have been hiding ever since. The fellowship with God that was the very purpose for Adam and Eve's existence (and ours) was horribly broken by sin. A Reconciler had to come to bridge the gap that now lay between man and God. Jesus came and filled that gap with his life, death, and resurrection so that we could once again enjoy the fellowship with God for which we were created.

This is the message of the gospel—that God is at work, through Christ, reconciling the world to himself. The Lord goes on to use that restored relationship to work change in us. As we are brought back into fellowship with him as his children, as citizens of his kingdom, and members of his body the church, he can bring about the heart change that is his goal. He justifies so that he might sanctify. He reconciles so that we might be partakers of his divine nature, holy as he is holy. As Christ's ambassadors, we must remember that this is the goal that should guide the words we speak to the people in our lives.

What does this mean practically? Yes, we want to solve the horizontal, earthly problems in our lives, but we want more than that. Human problems are opportunities God can use to draw the people around us into a fuller and deeper fellowship with him. This higher agenda is present in every relationship and every situation. God is working redemptively in all of them. We want our words to contribute to what he is doing. However, we will not be instruments of reconciliation if we are living in broken, unreconciled relationships with other people. We are called to speak words of peace, words that restore, and words that encourage fellowship and unity. We do this not just so we would be happy, but so that God would be able to work redemptively in the context of this unity and fellowship.

We are called to speak for the King. God has put us just where he wants us in order to make his appeal through us. We need to be committed to his higher agenda, living and speaking out of self-sacrificing love, humble forgiveness, and a commitment to reconciliation.

One of my most vivid learning experiences along these lines came during the early years of my pastoral ministry. My family lived in a twin home, with our landlady and her daughter living next door. For a while, our relationship was fine and living there was a pleasure. But then, for reasons we did not understand, things began to change. Bridget, our landlady's daughter, began to respond to us in anger whenever we saw her. She yelled at our children. She accused us of saying and doing things we did not do. She played her stereo as loudly as possible late at night, waking our children. Life quickly turned from pleasurable to intolerable.

We were living on a meager income and right after we had moved into the house, our refrigerator had broken down. Bridget had allowed us to borrow hers. It was now summer and my wife's parents had come to see us. In preparation for their visit, we had loaded the refrigerator with food. But the day after they arrived, we got a call from Bridget saying that she wanted her refrigerator back immediately. I asked if her mother's had broken. She told me that it hadn't, but that our refrigerator belonged to her and she wanted it back. I told her that it was full of food and asked her if we could return it in about a week. She said she wanted it back by five o'clock that day.

I was steaming by the time I got off the phone. This was the climax of all we had been enduring for the last few months, the final indignity! We took the food out of the refrigerator, placed it on the kitchen table in the heat of our ninety-degree, un-air-conditioned house, and returned the refrigerator to the garage. I walked out wishing that I would encounter Bridget because I had things to say to her! Thankfully, God had another plan.

That afternoon Luella was making bread, and as usual I asked her to make a batch of cinnamon rolls. As she was placing the rolls in the oven she turned to me and said, "You know, Paul, we ought to give a plate of these rolls to Bridget." (Yeah—exactly what I was thinking!) "God tells us that we should overcome evil with good and that we should look for ways to do good to those who mistreat us. Since I'm making the rolls, why don't you write a note to Bridget telling her how much we love her and desire to have a good relationship with her?" (Another brilliant idea, I thought!)

That was one of the hardest notes I have ever written. I was filled with my sense of being wronged. I wanted Bridget to hurt the way she had hurt us. I wanted her life to be as hard as ours had been over the previous months. I wanted her to feel what it was like to walk on eggshells all the time, only to be yelled at anyway. I found it hard to leave room for God's wrath (Rom. 12:19) because I was so filled with my own.

But by the grace of God I did what Luella suggested. I took the note and the plate of warm rolls over to the adjoining house. Our landlady answered the door. When I told her that the rolls were for her daughter, she told me that I must be some kind of nut. (She had been very embarrassed by her daughter's behavior.) I told her that I thought this was what God wanted me to do.

That plate of rolls represented our submission to God's mission and methods in the midst of personal difficulty. We looked for every opportunity to do good and to speak kindly to Bridget. We sought to love and serve wherever and whenever we could. Yes, the old anger would well up, but we continued to encourage one another to overcome evil with good.

It was late one autumn afternoon when I heard a knock at the door. When I saw it was Bridget, my heart sank. I thought, *What now? We have worked so hard to be nice!* When I got to the door I could see that Bridget was upset. She asked if she could come in and talk to us. Luella and I sat down with her as tears streamed down her cheeks. She said, "I know that I have been impossible to live with and that I have done many things to make your life difficult. I don't know why I have been so mean, so angry. I have alienated my family and all of my close friends. You are the only two people that I know for sure love me. I've come here because I need your help." In our dining room that afternoon, we talked with Bridget about the help that only Christ could give.

Luella had been right. She had seen God's agenda for our relationship with Bridget. My self-righteous, angry words would never have produced that scene. Allowing myself to be drawn into an ever-escalating war of words would not have produced it. I realized that afternoon that the whole situation had not been a mistake. We had not been in this trial because God had forgotten us. No, he had been at work all through it, sanctifying us, and he had also been at work *through* us. He had put us there as his ambassadors so that he might restore Bridget to himself. He called us to speak words of love and good, to speak out of hearts that were willing to die to self, willing to forgive, willing to be part of his work of reconciliation. And he gave us his Spirit to free us from the bondage to self so that our words *could* be gracious tools of change.

God calls each of us to live and speak as his ambassadors. We are on the job twenty-four hours a day. Everything we do and say reflects an awareness of the One we represent. God has called us to be part of an agenda higher than the horizontal need of the moment. We are called to carry his words of redemption into every situation of life.

Getting Personal: Speaking as an Ambassador

1. Where in your life do you find irritation, anger, or frustration that reveals a commitment to your own agenda and not the Lord's?

2. Where are your opportunities to be part of what God is doing in others?

3. In what situations do you tend to fight using the weapons of the world?

4. In what ways is God calling you to personal sacrifice in order to be his ambassador?

5. Are there people in your life that you have failed to forgive?

6. Where is God calling you to speak as an agent of reconciliation?

Chapter Eight

Getting to the Destination

My grace is enough; it's all you need. My strength comes into its own in your weakness. (2 Cor. 12:9)

WHEN I wrote this book, I was on sabbatical in Clearwater, Florida. A beautiful causeway with water on both sides connects Clearwater and the city of Tampa. I once commented to someone that Clearwater looked so beautiful from the Tampa side of the bay and that the causeway made getting there so easy. My companion then told me about a hurricane that once hit western Florida and left the Clearwater causeway completely under water. He said, "You could see Clearwater, you could describe it to someone, but you couldn't get there because the causeway was flooded."

Perhaps this is how you have felt about this book so far. I have described a destination to you, the world of talk as God has planned it, but you feel as if your causeway is flooded and there is no way to get there. Maybe you have seen more clearly than ever before how far your communication is from where God wants it to be. Unfortunately, this only leaves you feeling more hopeless than ever!

The purpose of this chapter is to calm the storm and give you a passable causeway. I want to give you hope and help. I want to help you begin to rebuild your world of talk.

Practical Steps to the Destination

1. *Don't give in to regret.* It is so easy to get swallowed up by remorse. It is easy to become paralyzed by "if onlys," and side-tracked by questioning God's timing. Here are some things we need to consider.

God is the Wonderful Counselor. He is the universe's best teacher. He knows exactly how much truth we are able to understand and to bear. One of the last things Christ said to his disciples was that there was much more that he had to say to them, but they were not able to bear it. He promised to send another teacher who would continue to instruct them. God always reveals truth to us at the right moment. There is never a mistake in his timing. Instead of regret, we need to rest in his sovereign wisdom.

Second, Scripture promises that God "will restore what the locusts have eaten" (Joel 2:25). It is important for us to remember that the God who forgives also restores, rebuilds, and reconciles. As we live in light of the new things he has taught us, we will experience restoration in places where we had long since given up. Through our present obedience to the new insights, God works to restore the damage done in the past. I have seen this take place again and again with parents, friends, and married couples who were tempted to believe that the damage of the past could never be undone.

2. *Embrace gospel hope.* We must not allow ourselves to look at our communication struggles as giants that cannot be defeated. Paul said to Timothy, "God did not give us a spirit of timidity, but a spirit of power, of love and of self-discipline" (2 Tim. 1:7). We get overwhelmed, fearful, and timid when we forget who we are in Christ.

We must first of all remember that we are the recipients of grace that abounds wherever our sin does. Yes, our sin will confound us, but it will not confound the Savior. His life, death, and resurrection guarantee victory. Romans 6:14 says,

"For sin shall not be your master, because you are not under law, but under grace." This grace is available to us in every situation and relationship of our lives, and it is made perfect in our weakness!

Second, we must remember that trouble does not mean that God has forsaken us. The psalmist reminds us in Psalm 46 that God is "an ever-present help in trouble." It is not enough to say that he cares for us in trouble or that he is available to help us in trouble. No, he is more. He is there *in* the trouble as a refuge and strength. We are never without a place of protection and never without a source of strength because God is always near!

Third, God knew that our condition as sinners was so desperate and his calling so high that forgiveness would not be enough. He follows his forgiveness by literally getting inside us in the person of his Spirit. Paul captures this amazing reality with these words, "Now to him who is able to do immeasurably more than all we ask or imagine, according to his power that is *at work within us*" (Eph. 3:20). His power is not only *in* us, it is *at work*! Yes, he forgives, but he also empowers. He will not call us to do anything without giving us what we need to do it. If the Lord calls you to cross the Red Sea, he will send a boat, build a bridge, part the waters, or help you swim!

3. *Examine your fruit.* What is the fruit produced by your communication? Do you leave others encouraged, hopeful, and loved? Do your words lead to forgiveness, reconciliation, and peace? Does your communication impart wisdom and encourage faith? Or do your words lead to discouragement, division, condemnation, bitterness, and foolishness?

Change begins with a humble willingness to examine your harvest. Galatians 6:7 says, "Do not be deceived; God cannot be mocked. A man reaps what he sows." One of the cruel tricks of the enemy is to convince us that our harvest really belongs to someone else. ("He makes me so angry!" "I never had a problem with my words until I had children." "If you had my husband, you'd yell too!" "My boss always brings out the worst in me.")

Take courage in the Lord's promise of forgiveness and his powerful presence; then examine the fruit of your words. Own your harvest before the Lord. It is here that lasting change will begin.

4. *Uncover your roots.* Luke 6:45 records one of the most important things that Christ said about our communication, "For out of the overflow of his heart his mouth speaks." Word problems always point to heart problems. Examining where we have trouble with our talk will reveal what is ruling our hearts.

When I was growing up, my parents would take us to family reunions on my mom's side of the family. My mother's brothers and sisters were all unbelievers. Whenever we went to one of these reunions, my parents would stay for the meal and then whisk us away before the drinking began.

At one reunion my mom was engaged in conversation and did not realize that my uncle had gotten drunk in another room, where he was saying sexually provocative things about the women present in front of me and my brother Mark. When Mom realized what was happening, she ran in, grabbed our hands, and stuffed us in the car. On the way home she said, "There is nothing that comes out of a drunk that wasn't there in the first place." I will never forget those words.

We must begin by admitting that people and situations do not cause us to speak as we do. Our hearts control our words. People and situations simply provide the occasion for the heart to express itself. Humbly confessing this opens to you the floodgates of God's forgiveness and power. "He is faithful and just and will forgive us our sins and purify us from all unrighteousness" (1 John 1:9).

5. *Seek forgiveness.* The old proverb says that confession is good for the soul. How true! You see, if your heart has been ex-

posed to truth and you have thought, done, or said what is wrong, you only have two options. You can confess your sin and place yourself once again under the forgiving grace of Christ, or you can erect some system of self-justification that makes what God calls sin acceptable to your conscience. How good we are at doing this! We recast events. ("I wasn't really angry, I was trying to emphasize my point.") We blame others. ("She has a unique ability to drive me crazy!") We claim physical weakness. ("I wasn't feeling well, so I just wasn't myself.") We appeal to the situation. ("It was just one of those days!") All this is done in an attempt to excuse what God says is inexcusable.

What is the fruit of this? Proverbs says it well: "He who conceals his sins does not prosper" (Prov. 28:13). Seeking forgiveness is like weeding a garden. It leaves the soil of the soul free to grow the new life of obedience. The weeds of unconfessed sin choke out the life of the soul.

A major part of rebuilding your world of talk is to ask yourself the question, What specific sins of communication (both heart and mouth—see Luke 6:46) is the Lord calling me to confess to him or to others? In asking this question you are keeping in step with the Spirit, who is working to conform you to the image of the Son (Gal. 5:16–26). And in so doing, you are clearing the soil of the soul so that the Spirit may plant the seeds of the character of Christ.

Seeking forgiveness is a significant turning point. Here we quit fighting against what the Lord is seeking to do in our lives and become cooperative, submissive participants. The result always is a harvest of good fruit. Our souls become a garden for his glory and our mouths become an orchard filled with the sweet fruit of the Spirit (words of love, joy, peace, patience, kindness, goodness, faithfulness, gentleness, and self-control).

6. *Freely grant forgiveness.* There are two aspects to this step of the rebuilding process. First, there must be *judicial* forgiveness. This is our willingness to let go of another's offense be-

fore God. It is, in actuality, surrendering to God any right or desire for vengeance. Paul says, "Do not take revenge, my friends, but leave room for God's wrath, for it is written, 'It is mine to avenge; I will repay,' says the Lord" (Rom. 12:19).

When God says, "Leave room for my wrath," he is essentially saying, "Stay out of my way and let me do my job." Forgiveness starts vertically. It is handing the offense over to the Lord and resting in his justice.

The second aspect of forgiveness is *relational* forgiveness. This is the willingness to forgive anyone who comes seeking it. "Be kind and compassionate to one another, forgiving each other, just as in Christ God forgave you" (Eph. 4:32).

In my counseling experience I have seen that there is no greater impediment to change than the unwillingness to seek and grant forgiveness. The lack of forgiveness causes us to fight God rather than submit to him and causes us to stand against rather than with one another.

7. *Change the rules.* A commitment to a new way of speaking needs to follow the sweet obedience of forgiveness. This new commitment needs to be as specific as the sin that was confessed. What is God calling you to change in your communication? What new ways of speaking must replace the old patterns?

When couples have confessed their sins in this way, I encourage them to set new goals for their communication. I ask them to agree to cry "Foul!" when one of them gives in to the old way for a moment. I suggest that they agree to raise their hand in the middle of a conversation and say, "We agreed not to speak to each other this way. Let's stop and pray and then try to have this conversation in a way that pleases the Lord." I have seen this strategy alone radically renew the communication of a husband and wife.

The "put off" of confession and repentance must be followed by the "put on" of a specific, practical commitment to a new way of talking. This commitment to change the rules is rooted in a living faith in Scripture (What it calls me to is right and best) and a living faith in the presence of the Lord (He is with me wherever I go, supplying everything I need to do what he has called me to do; see 2 Peter 1:3–9).

8. *Look for opportunities.* This is not so much a change of direction as it is a change of perspective. Those situations that were the source of difficulty, those moments where unkind, selfish, and ungodly words were spoken, those situations you once dreaded, now become opportunities to experience the enabling grace of the Lord and exercise newfound character and obedience.

As you forsake regret, bathe yourself in the gospel, face your sin, and seek and grant forgiveness, you will get a vision for a whole new life of communication. You will not look at life as a dangerous jungle filled with ravenous animals, poisonous snakes, and hidden pools of quicksand. No, you will look at life as a garden of opportunity in which you can actually experience the wonderful things God has planned for his children.

Proverbs 28:1 says, "The wicked man flees though no one pursues, but the righteous are as bold as a lion." Go out with the boldness of a lion. Refuse to give in any longer to cynicism and fear. Refuse to give in to dread, doubt, and avoidance. Live boldly. Capture redemptive opportunities. Seize the promised provisions of the Lord. He will give you many opportunities to speak in a new way!

9. *Choose your words.* Proverbs says, "The heart of the righteous weighs its answers" (Prov. 15:28). We are told in Proverbs that it is folly to speak in haste. As we begin to look for God-given opportunities to speak in a new way, we must learn to think before we speak. We must learn to choose our words wisely. The final section of this book will discuss in detail what this means. I have heard so many people say in regret, "I wish I hadn't spoken so soon," or "I just got carried away," or "I wish I could take those words back."

God has chosen our words to run on two tracks. The first is the track of his glory. The words of our mouths must first be acceptable to him. The second is the track of our neighbor's good. God's call is that we would choose words that travel well on these tracks.

10. *Confess your weakness.* One of the sure signs that we have not really understood the gospel is when we continue to be afraid of, discouraged by, and unwilling to accept our weakness. Christ came precisely because we *are* weak! There is no indication in Scripture that we will ever outgrow our need of his moment-by-moment supply of grace. If we obey him for a thousand years, we will need him just as much then as we did the first day we believed!

The awareness of weakness, rather than being a sure sign of immaturity, is actually the sign of the opposite. The closer we get to the Lord, the longer we walk with him, and the more fully we understand his Word, the more we are gripped with our weakness, inability, and sin. Paul said that he "would boast all the more gladly" about his weakness (2 Cor. 12:9). It was not because he loved being weak, but because it was in weakness that the power of Christ rested on him. Our weakness will not get in the way of what the Lord wants to do in us. Our delusions of strength will! The power of God is for the weak! The grace of God is for the unable! The promises of God are for the faint! The wisdom of God is for the foolish!

Because of his grace, in our weakness, inability, faintheartedness, and foolishness, we are free to run to him rather than run from him. We really can come to him just as we are. No place better demonstrates our need of him than our moment-by-moment struggles with words. Embrace your weakness and run with joy to the only Source of strength.

11. *Don't give the Devil an opportunity.* As Paul talks about our communication in Ephesians 4, he says, "Do not give the devil an opportunity." Satan is a liar and a trickster. He

seeks to divide and destroy. He is the enemy of all that is good and right. He seeks to sow the weeds of doubt, despair, and rebellion. He hates living faith. He fights new life. He seeks to turn us from God and against one another. We must be wise to his tricks and do anything we can to keep him from having his way with us. We must forbid him any room to work.

In our life of talk there are two things we can do that will shut the door to Satan and his cruel work. First, we can commit ourselves to the *courage of honesty*. A commitment to loving truthfulness is a wonderful safeguard from the destructive work of the enemy. He lives in the darkness. He works in our silence. When we bring issues into the light, when we put them on the table, we give him little room to work.

Second, we need to commit ourselves to the *humility of approachability*. A commitment to speak truthfully when coupled with a humble willingness to listen will close the door on Satan's foot. Much of our communication trouble results when we unwittingly give the Devil an opportunity.

The Blessing of God's Way

Early in our relationship Luella and I realized that communication would be one of our areas of difficulty. Luella was from a very well-mannered, soft-spoken family. The rule in her home was to never say anything that could be remotely considered controversial. If a disagreement would erupt, someone would quickly change the subject.

I grew up in a family where everyone spoke at once. Conversations regularly escalated to higher volumes. The rule in our family was to speak quickly without thinking or you might lose your opportunity to speak at all!

As you can imagine, this communication mix was poisonous to us as a young couple. Both of us struggled with anger— Luella clamming up while I was blowing up. It wasn't long before we were both very discouraged. One simple principle brought change and new life to our communication. We were reading Ephesians and came across this verse, "Do not let the sun go down while you are still angry" (4:26). We both had one of those "well duh!" moments! Of course! It is a very simple yet elegant direction.

We determined that we would not go to sleep at night without dealing with the things that had happened that day. The first few nights we stubbornly lay in bed, propping our eyes open as we waited for the other to make the first move! What we hadn't realized is that to obey the principle you not only have to deal with your words, but you have to deal with your heart as well. This is where the war is really taking place. But we began to see the wonderful benefit of doing it God's way. It wasn't long before we weren't waiting until evening. We began seeking one another out shortly after we had spoken unkindly, asking for forgiveness. We are now at the place where we can't wait to seek forgiveness and restore our relationship.

Speaking Out of Hope

But you may be thinking, *Paul, you don't know how bad it is for us. It seems hopeless!* I urge you not to look at the giant of your communication problems as the army of Israel did Goliath, comparing their size to his. Look at your communication problems with the eyes of David, comparing puny Goliath to the awesome grandeur and glory of God. He is able! He is the great Author of change! He is the Restorer! There is life in his Words! He will not call you to anything that he does not enable you to do!

Remember the core perspectives of this book:

- God has a wonderful plan for our words that is far better than anything we could come up with on our own.

- Sin has radically altered our agenda for our words, resulting in much hurt, confusion, and chaos.
- In Christ Jesus we find the grace that provides all that we need to speak as God has planned.
- The Bible plainly and simply teaches us how to get from where we are to where God wants us to be.

We can reach Clearwater! We don't have to gaze at its beauty discouraged because the causeway is flooded! God has given us everything we need to dry out and rebuild the road to God-honoring, people-benefiting communication. We need to step forward in the courage of faith, confessing our sin and weakness and embracing the hope found only in his forgiving and enabling grace.

Leave regret behind. Grab hold of the hope found in the presence and work of Jesus. Examine the fruit of your communication and trace that fruit back to root issues in the heart. Seek and grant forgiveness, not just once but as a moment-by-moment pattern. Agree with those around you to change the rules. Put down the old human way; it really does lead to death. Take up with joy the wonderful commands and principles of the Word. Look for opportunities to apply the new things God is teaching you about his way of communication. With joy speak words that have been chosen because they are acceptable to the Lord and beneficial to others. Be ready and willing every day to confess your weakness. This is the secret to experiencing his strength. Finally, refuse to give the Devil an opportunity. Be courageously honest. Be humbly approachable. Don't give the Devil any dark hallways or silent rooms in which to work.

Remember that God knows what you need. If the enemy is too strong, God will defeat him. If you are facing the Red Sea, he will part the waters. If you are thirsty and without water, he will bring it out of a rock. If you are hungry, he will provide manna. If you have sinned, he will forgive. If you are weak, he will empower. The Redeemer has come! There is hope for our talk!

Getting Personal: Rebuilding the Causeway

1. Where have you been tempted to believe Satan's discouraging lies? ("He/she/they'll never change! It is impossible to forgive him/her/them after the horrible things they've said. God doesn't really care about your communication; he has better, more important things to do. Your anger really isn't your fault. If others lived where you do, they would be angry too! Being humble just gives people an opportunity to take advantage of you," etc.)

2. What communication regrets do you need to leave behind? What "if onlys" have gotten in the way of the change to which God has called you?

3. What specific verbal sins do you need to confess? To whom?

4. Which of God's promises do you need to remember daily so that you will have hope in the midst of the struggle?

5. Where do you need to start right now, as you seek to cooperate with God who is willing and able to restore your world of talk? What immediate changes is he calling you to?

Chapter Nine

Citizens in Need of Help

Watch your step, friends. Make sure there's no evil unbelief lying around that will trip you up and throw you off course. . . . Keep each other on your toes so sin doesn't slow down your reflexes.

(Heb. 3:12–13)

HAVE you ever been asked to do something that you really didn't want to do? You know, one of those jobs that you put off again and again, that you do only when your back is against the wall and you really have no other options? Most of us feel this way about confrontation. The very word sounds ominous to us. In our minds we picture a tense conversation, glaring eyes, pointed fingers, raised voices, red faces, and inflammatory words. This is not a scene that warms us with anticipation!

If I asked to come over to your house tomorrow and rebuke you, would you be excited? Would you say to your spouse or friend, "I just got great news! Paul is coming over tomorrow to rebuke me! I can't wait—I haven't been rebuked for so long! It's about time!" No, we treat confrontation and rebuke with the anticipation we reserve for a root canal. Yet Scripture tells us that this ministry is an essential part of God's plan for our words.

Why Is Confrontation So Scary?

The easiest answer to this question is that, as sinners, we spend much of our time hiding from, excusing, or blaming others for our sin. Scripture says, "Men loved darkness instead of light because their deeds were evil" (John 3:19). Surely, this is true. Sinners (and that includes us all) don't tend to be comfortable when their lives are under inspection. We tend to be better at seeing the speck in the eye of our neighbor than we are at seeing the log in our own eye.

But there is more going on here. Yes, we dread confrontation because we don't like to look at our sin, but we also dread confrontation because of the troublesome and unbiblical way we've seen it handled. There are legitimate reasons for our dread of rebuke.

Let me suggest several ways in which our agenda for confrontation gets confused with the Lord's.

1. *Confrontation often confuses personal irritation and anger with biblical perspectives and purposes.* As we will see later, the purpose of confrontation is not to arrange for our opinions to dominate someone else's. It is not to let another person "have it" when we've had enough. Confrontation usually occurs when someone has sinned or hurt and offended someone else. But biblical priorities in such a situation often get crowded out by our frustration with the person whose sin has affected us. He or she has made our lives difficult. So our anger distorts the issues that need to be addressed, and the time of confrontation itself is clouded by our frustration.

2. *Poor data gathering can lead to incorrect assumptions about the facts, which derails confrontation.* The first important step of confrontation is data gathering. We need to make sure that we see the issues accurately. We need to be sure that the person is guilty of the charge. Otherwise, a distorted perspective will

cloud confrontation. We must be careful that what we think we see is in fact what has happened.

3. *Confrontation is often marred by a judgment of motives.* In times of rebuke, we tend to talk not only about what the person did but also about the reasons behind his or her actions. Unfortunately, this often results in the person being misunderstood and wrongly accused. There are times when we are right in pointing out areas of failure, but we then improperly judge the person for motives that really were not there! In such a case, the person who is accused will miss the accurate part of the message that he or she needed to hear.

4. *Inflammatory language, condemning words, and emotional tones often stain confrontation.* In confrontation the air is often thick with tension. Things are said more as angry judgments than the gentle but unwavering words of rebuke that Scripture enjoins. In these situations, the person being confronted will forget the message and remember the angry words and tones that controlled the moment.

5. *Confrontations are often adversarial rather than moments of loving concern for the person who needs your rebuke.* In confrontation we can forget who we are. We can fail to remember that we would be exactly where the other person is if not for God's grace. We seem to forget that, really, there is only one enemy—and it is not the person being confronted! The purpose of confrontation is not to stand against the person, but to stand alongside him, pointing out the things God wants him to see, confess, and forsake.

6. *In confrontation, Scripture is often used more as a club than as a mirror of self-awareness and a guide to change.* In rebuke the most important use of Scripture is not its warning of punishment, but the powerful way it functions as a mirror. Scripture enables people to see themselves as they really are. It exposes the wrong

not only in a person's behavior but in the person's heart as well. The primary goal of confrontation is not to threaten a person with judgment, but to lead him to confession.

7. *Confrontation often confuses human expectations with God's will.* The purpose of confrontation is not to get someone to do what you want or to live in a way that pleases you. The goal of rebuke is not to get a person to agree with you, to submit to your interpretation, or to follow your agenda. Confrontation should always call a person to submit to the will of God alone.

8. *Confrontation often takes place in the context of a broken relationship.* Often there has already been a damaging distance between the parties involved before the confrontation takes place. Both people enter the room nursing their wounds and already feeling a little negative toward the other. This sets the confrontation in the wrong direction before it has even begun. Confrontation is most effective in the context of a relationship where love and trust are mutually understood. This way, confrontation can indeed be the "faithful wounds of a friend."

9. *Confrontation often demands that change be an immediate event rather than a process.* Many times in confrontation we fail to give the Spirit room to work. Nothing in Scripture tells us to expect a person to undergo a complete reversal of heart and behavior after one meeting. In fact, the Bible depicts change more as a process than as an event. We are meant to call a person to submit to the Lord and to obey his Word without applying undue pressure, as if we can do the work of the Spirit.

The Fruit of Confrontation Gone Wrong

We have all been negatively affected by these errors. These tend to be the things that produce a feeling of dread whenever confrontation is mentioned. Like the appointment with the dentist, we tend to play out in our minds all of the worst-case scenarios we can imagine, and we try to plan what we will do if this or that scenario takes place. Not only do we dread being on the receiving end of confrontation, but most of us dread being the confronter. We fret about whether we will have the right things to say, whether we will find the right time and place, how our words will be received, and what will be left of the relationship when the confrontation is over. Most of us on both sides find these moments to be unnatural, tense, and uncomfortable. So, as citizens in the kingdom of God, we tend to avoid confrontation whenever and however possible.

I remember being asked by a pastor to attend a meeting where he would be confronting a member of his congregation. (I had previously been this man's counselor.) The evening had an almost surreal quality to it. The first thing that struck me was the pained, unnatural greetings between the pastor, the elders, and this man. These men had all once shared a close relationship. There was an attempt to be personable and warm, but it came across as labored and difficult. When all the "safe" things had been said, we sat in the room, staring into the silence for what seemed an eternity. No one seemed relaxed, no one had a smile or even a pleasant expression on his face, and no one made eye contact with anyone else. I wanted to stand up and scream, "What is going on here? This is not the way it is supposed to be!" But I restrained myself(!).

The pastor suggested that we start with prayer and he led us. He seemed no more comfortable as he prayed than he had during those initial greetings. He then said, "You know what we're here for, Bob. We're here to talk to you about some things that have been concerning us for a long time." Bob sat there no doubt wishing he were at the dentist. The pastor then pulled from his briefcase six typed pages of charges against this man and began to read, verbatim, through the list. There was no discussion, no interchange. Bob just sat there squirming as charge after charge was read. When the final page had been completed, Bob was asked if he was ready to confess and repent of these things. Bob seemed confused, hurt, and angry. The pastor glared at him like a judge on his bench.

At that point I could restrain myself no longer. I jumped in and asked if I could make a few suggestions (using basic principles of confrontation we will consider later in this chapter). I hoped that somehow we could regroup and get something of lasting benefit out of this horribly uncomfortable moment.

A Very Different Way

I've thought back to that evening many, many times. No wonder there is such a negative response to the mention of confrontation and rebuke! Sin is hard to admit and talk about, but our approach to it has made it even more difficult. Consequently, much that needs to be brought into the light never sees the light of day until it has grown so serious that it cannot be ignored. Issues that were once small and simple are now huge and complicated, and the process of confrontation is much more difficult.

Whenever I think of confrontation, my mind goes to Nathan (2 Sam. 12). What a job he had to do! Nathan was called by God to confront King David. This story is instructive for us. First, we ought to be impressed that David needed to be confronted at all! It was not as if the issues Nathan was called to deal with were subtle ones like pride or selfishness, things that can be hard to see. David had committed adultery and murder!

It also ought to impress us that Nathan is confronting *David,* the anointed king of Israel. This is a man who had been schooled in the things of God from the time of his birth. Surely David knew the law of the Lord. Why wasn't he conscience-stricken? Why wasn't he eaten up with conviction of sin? Why did he need someone to stand before him and point out what should have been blatantly obvious?

Herein lies the significance of this story. It gives us a real window into the heart of man, and God's covenant commitment to intervene in our blindness and rebellion with his redemptive grace. David had taken another man's wife as his own, had her husband killed, and returned unrepentant to his duties as God's appointed leader. Not until Nathan told him the wonderful story of the poor man and his one little ewe lamb did David see the heinous nature of his sin against God, Uriah, Bathsheba, and the people of Israel. What a glaring example of the deceitfulness of the heart! What a powerful reminder of our need for intervention! We, too, are capable of living with sin against God and others. We, too, are capable of going on as if nothing has happened and we are okay. We, too, need God to raise up people who are willing to accept the hard job of helping us to see ourselves as God does. This is what this chapter is about—re-examining the nature of the intervention God calls us to make in each other's lives. What is the nature of our need, and what kind of help has God called us to give each other?

Even though we have been transported from the dominion of darkness to the kingdom of light, as believers we are still *citizens in need of help*. We do not want to minimize the significance of our rescue from the domain of darkness into the kingdom of God's Son, but this deliverance is not the *end* of Christ's work of salvation; it is the *beginning*. Once he has broken the dominion of darkness *over* us, he then begins to remove all the darkness *within* us so that we may be holy as he is holy. This is the ongoing work of his kingdom rule—our sanctification. All of the writers of the Epistles recognize the glory of our justification, but they also recognize the utter necessity of our ongoing sanctification. (See Rom. 8 and 1 Peter 1 for two classic examples of this balance.)

As we consider the primary focus of God's kingdom work

(our sanctification) we get an even more detailed understanding of what God has called us to in our communication.
Here again, we find biblical guardrails for all that we say to
one another. Our speaking must have the principal work of
God's kingdom in view. The battle is not over yet. Sin's dominion has been broken, but the darkness within must be exposed and rooted out wherever it exists. Our talk with one another has been ordained by God to be a vital part of that work.
The radical stance of the New Testament is that intervention
is not limited to occasional moments of confrontation. Rather,
it is a lifestyle, a commitment that shapes all of our interactions as members of the body of Christ. This is the new and
higher agenda that makes our talk very different from the talk
of the world. In some way our talk should always have ongoing
redemption in view. It always goes beyond the surface, horizontal issues of the moment. It always has a vertical dimension.

Maybe you're wondering, *Are we never supposed to deal with
the real stuff of life—the nasty comment, the unpaid bill, the broken
promise, the family squabble, the inattentive husband, the nagging
wife, the car left without gas once again, the loud rock music, the controlling elder, the fight over the bathroom, etc.? Are we called to minister all the time?* The issue is not *whether* you deal with these
things—you must. The issue is *how*. Because of indwelling sin
and God's ongoing work of sanctification, we are called to communication that has a goal higher than solving the problem of
the moment. We must see our words as his tools. So we seek to
solve the problem of the moment in a way that propels the
work God is doing through it. The recognition of the reality of
indwelling sin is a key element in a life of God-honoring talk.

Your Talk and Sin's Deceitfulness

Let me take you to a powerful passage that displays what
happens to our communication when we acknowledge indwelling sin.

See to it, brothers, that none of you has a sinful, unbelieving heart that turns away from the living God. But encourage one another daily, as long as it is called Today, so that none of you may be hardened by sin's deceitfulness. We have come to share in Christ if we hold firmly till the end the confidence we had at first. As has just been said:

> *"Today, if you hear his voice,*
> *do not harden your hearts*
> *as you did in the rebellion." (Heb. 3:12–15)*

This passage does more than cause us to sit up and take notice. It also gives us real guidance as to what it means practically to speak as an ambassador of the Lord. It acknowledges the harsh realities of life in God's kingdom. The battle is not over; the work is not done. We are all citizens who need help and are called to give it. Any other perspective on the Christian life does not do this passage justice.

Notice the way this passage warns against the danger of wandering away from the Lord. The old familiar hymn says:

> *O to grace how great a debtor*
> *Daily I'm constrained to be!*
> *Let Thy goodness, like a fetter,*
> *Bind my wandering heart to Thee:*
> *Prone to wander, Lord, I feel it,*
> *Prone to leave the God I love;*
> *Here's my heart, O take and seal it;*
> *Seal it for Thy courts above.*

This hymn echoes the warning so powerfully given in the Hebrews passage. We have been rescued, but we are still prone to wander away from our Rescuer. Even though we are citizens in the Son's kingdom, our wandering days are not over.

We wander away when we express the anger we feel toward our spouse or children. We wander away when we covet the blessing of a friend. We wander away when we compromise biblical conviction for acceptance, for possessions, or for position. We wander away when we surrender to a moment of lust. We wander away when we doubt God and his goodness. We wander away when we have opportunity to be salt and light, but remain silent and inactive, when the cares of this world squeeze out a diligent pursuit of God. Wandering does not only refer to rank apostasy. Much of our wandering is subtle and unnoticed. This is why we need one another.

Notice also that this passage speaks to believers, to "brothers." Four words are used in this passage to describe this wandering away of the believer: *sinful, unbelieving, turning away,* and *hardened* heart. The writer is describing something more fundamental than the committing of specific sins. He is warning us against a subtle turn of the heart from God, which results in a change in the way we see God and ourselves. This, in turn, results in a radical difference in the way we live our lives.

There is a progressive character to this string of words that describes the turning away of the believer. The *sinful* heart, not wanting to live under the convicting light of truth, lives in the shadows and becomes weak and *unbelieving.* The unbelieving heart, having lost its confidence in God, has no reason to continue to persevere and begins to *turn away.* And the heart that has turned away, no longer sensitive to the truth of God, becomes increasingly *hardened* to the things of the Lord. What the passage describes is a subtle acceptance of sin patterns, an acceptance that grows until it becomes a hardened turning away from the living God. What a terrifying warning!

Perhaps you are asking yourself at this point, How could this happen to a believer? After all Christ has done for him, how could a believer become so hardened? This question gets to the heart of the warning and the passage. When we answer this question, we will also get a sense of God's practical, everyday agenda for our talk.

This horrifying progression in a believer's life is explained by a little phrase that is probably the key phrase in the passage. The passage says that we can become hardened "by sin's deceitfulness." There is a world of theology hidden within this little phrase. Sin is by its very nature deceitful. The heart is by its very nature deceitful (see Jer. 17:9). The writer of Hebrews is alerting us to the reality of the spiritual blindness that exists to some degree in the life of every sinner. We do not see ourselves as we need to. Sin is deceitful—and guess who it deceives first? I have no trouble seeing the sins of my wife and my children; their sins are obvious to me. Yet I am regularly surprised when mine are pointed out! And too often, when my sin has been confronted, I am tempted to conclude that I have not sinned. Rather, my actions and motives have been once again misunderstood. This, my friends, is spiritual blindness, and all of us suffer from it to some degree.

If you accept this reality, it will change the way you think about the Christian life and your relationships. Being a Christian does not mean that we are free of spiritual blindness or the potential for self-deception. As long as there is indwelling sin, spiritual blindness and self-deception will exist. It is because of this reality that the writer says that we need one another daily. You see me in ways that I will not see myself. As you walk in the truth, you can bring a level of clarity to me that I would not have alone. I need your daily encouragement so that indwelling sin would not blind me. Your encouragement is a principal means that God uses to keep me from sin and unbelief.

As a young pastor, I got a call one afternoon from a couple who had attended our church. They were desperate for help and wanted their situation to change. Yet at the same time they were victims of their own blindness. That night I sat in their living room and listened to their sad story; her slide into a paralyzing depression, his growing addiction to drugs and alcohol, and four children who seemed increasingly out of control. What impressed me that night was that, when viewed from their perspective, life gave them little reason to continue. They were blind to two fundamental realities that would form the substance of my ministry to them.

First, they were blind to themselves. They did not see that they were now harvesting the seeds they had planted. So there seemed to be no way out. Second, they were blind to the powerful presence of the Lord. So they felt helpless and hopeless. My calling was to be used of God to open their eyes to these two realities, and in so doing, give them powerful, solid reasons to continue. We all need this ministry so that we would not give way to sin and unbelief.

What does this mean practically? It means that none of us, this side of heaven, can say that we don't need help. Even citizens of the kingdom of light need the daily intervention of fellow citizens! Notice, too, that we are not called to exhort and encourage one another daily because of a particular sin we have seen someone commit. We are not called here to be spiritual detectives, trying to get the "goods" on one another. We are not being called to catch someone in sin. No, the reason for this daily ministry is not a specific *act* of sin, but the overall *condition* of spiritual blindness that results from the deceitfulness of sin. We suffer from this condition even when we are not committing sins that are obvious and visible to others. This means that, this side of eternity, there is never a moment when I do not need your help! I need your daily ministry to me as long as sin remains within me.

The Presence and Power of Indwelling Sin

I believe that the church of Jesus Christ seriously underestimates the power and presence of indwelling sin and its effect on our spiritual life. Remember, although we have been rescued from the kingdom of darkness, God is still working to remove the darkness within us. (See Rom. 7:14–25 for a gripping picture of indwelling sin and the resulting war within.)

When we do battle with sin in others and in ourselves, our

intervention is not meant to be critical or judgmental. It is intended to point us to Christ and the glories of his grace so that we would be encouraged to follow more humbly, carefully, and faithfully.

Each One a Helper, Each Needing Help

Did you notice that there are no *haves* and *have-nots* in this Hebrews passage? Instead, it describes humble, mutual, interdependent, peer ministry. Each believer is called to humbly recognize his daily need for help and each believer is called daily to be one of God's helpers. We all are helpers in need of help! We are each called to serve and to be willing to *be* served. In fact, this humble recognition of our own need is what enables us to be God's instruments of encouragement to others. We come recognizing that we need everything that we have come to give.

The ministry described in this passage cannot be left to the professional clergy. There is no way that there will ever be enough trained and ordained men to meet the "everyone–everyday" nature of this calling. It is a call that encompasses every member of the body of Christ. God's plan is that the professional clergy concentrate on training and equipping every member of the body of Christ for this essential ministry. It is also clear that this ministry will not primarily take place in the regular, formal gatherings of the church. It is most needed (and most successful) in the mundane moments of life. I need your encouragement along the way, as I am doing what God has called me to do in my personal, family, church, and community life. I need you to encourage me to hold on and to persevere.

There is one other thing to say about this important passage. It is not only a *warning*; it is a *call*. The turning point of this passage is a command—a command to communicate to one another with a certain *frequency, spirit,* and *message.* If we understand these three elements, we will begin to understand God's agenda for our talk. Let's consider each in turn.

Frequency:
An Everyday Readiness

When you think of ministry—how it is done and who does it—what comes to your mind? Perhaps you immediately think of the "professional" ministers, that is, the professionally trained (and paid) pastor, counselor, evangelist, and missionary. Perhaps your mind goes to all of the programmed opportunities for ministry in your local church: the Sunday morning worship service, Sunday school, the new members' class, the discipleship class, the home group meeting, Saturday afternoon evangelism teams, the nursing home ministry, short-term mission trips, the women's group, the men's fellowship, and the youth group. We should surely be thankful for these programs, but the writer of Hebrews sees the ministry of the body of Christ in much more robust and comprehensive terms. His view is nothing short of *everyone ministering everyday!*

This astounding call to daily ministry is necessary because of what we are dealing with. It reflects the universal spiritual struggle of all sinners. As long as sin remains in us, there will be some degree of deceitfulness in our hearts, with a resulting spiritual blindness. We carry this with us wherever we go. This means that in every situation, to every person, daily ministry is needed. This call extends far beyond the scheduled gatherings of the body of Christ.

Thus we recognize that our talk is meant to be a tool by which God protects us, not just from the temptations of external evil, but literally from ourselves! When a mother is in the kitchen discussing the school day with her son, she is doing more than getting a news report. She is looking for those spontaneous, God-given openings to encourage commitment to Christ. There is a friend at the coffee shop with his buddy, but he is doing more than talking about the news, the weather, sports, and the job market. He has submitted to God's call: he has accepted the harsh reality of the Christian life, and he is looking for opportunities to encourage hope in Christ. A husband and wife are out on a date, but they remain open to this higher calling because they have recognized their mutual spiritual need.

What all of these people have in common is an attitude of readiness. They all see ministry in much broader terms than the formal opportunities that church programs afford. And they are prepared to make the most of the opportunities God gives them every day. They really do believe that every day is a day for ministry. They understand the implications of being sinners; they embrace the fact that God places them just where he wants them to be used as his instruments; and they see their own need and are ready to be ministered to as well. Theirs is an *everyone, everyday* view of ministry. They rejoice in the fact that they are citizens in the kingdom of light, but they recognize at the same time that we are all citizens still in need of help.

Spirit:
The Humility of the Gospel

The spirit that underlies God's plan for our talk is the spirit of *humility*. That is the only appropriate response to the gospel realities revealed by this passage. In the gospel, the magnitude of our sin and the grandeur of God's grace are revealed. These realities leave no room for boasting (see Rom. 3:23 34, 27 28; 1 Cor. 1:26–31, Gal. 6:15; Eph. 2:8–9).

This humility echoes the spirit of Paul, who saw himself as the worst of all sinners (1 Tim. 1:15–17). It recognizes not only the grace given at conversion, but the daily grace that flows into our lives so that we may live and speak as God has planned.

An everyday ministry of intervention is not born out of

the pride of personal accomplishment, experience, wisdom, or success. Nor is it born out of a subtle belief that the persons giving and receiving ministry are somehow essentially different from each other. Rather, it admits that there is nothing that I can give another that I do not need myself. I may have known the Lord for many years, but I need his grace as much today as I did the first moment I believed. If there is any truth, life, hope, grace, and good in my life, it is because of his work. The only thing I bring to the table is my weakness and my sin. So I do not approach ministry from a position of confidence in my own strength and wisdom, encouraging you to be like me. No, I come in weakness and sin, to lead you to the only One who has strength and deliverance to offer!

When Paul describes the communication of the body of Christ, he always has this spirit in mind:

> *As a prisoner for the Lord, then, I urge you to live a life worthy of the calling you have received. Be completely humble and gentle; be patient, bearing with one another in love. (Eph. 4:1–2)*

Humility means acknowledging that I can offer only one thing that will help—Jesus Christ. There is a kindness, compassion, and gentleness that flows out of recognizing that we are brothers and sisters in the struggle, and that his grace *is* our only hope.

The Message: Encouragement to Persevere

The message we are called to bring to these everyday opportunities is this: *Don't give up! There is reason to continue! Be encouraged! Don't turn away! Believe in God's promises! Be tender in heart and keep following the Lord!* The message is not just confrontational. It is not a message of judgment, criticism, or condemnation. We are called to do more than point out another's sin. We are called to encourage faithfulness in battle until the victory is won.

Every one of God's war-weary soldiers needs this ministry of encouragement. We are all, at times, like the young child embarking on a long family trip who asks after three miles on the road, "Are we almost there, Daddy?" We all have to face the discouraging reality that the trip has only just begun. Life is a long journey. The Christian life is a long war. We all lose sight of our goal. We all go through times when it all seems too big and too hard. We all go through periods when we simply want to quit. We all have wandering hearts.

I once sat in my office with a father and his teenage son. I had witnessed the scene many times before. Neither wanted to be there. The father did not think he needed any help; he had only come as a way to get his son there. The son, meanwhile, sat slouched down in his chair and stared at the floor. He gave no indication that he was ready to be a participant. I could almost feel the anger between them. There was no warmth, no friendliness, and no familial love. They were trapped in their relationship and they both hated it.

The father spoke first. It didn't take long for his face to redden and his voice to rise. Although I had asked him a question, he spoke directly to his son. "I've fed and clothed you. I've taken you on great vacations. I did Little League and swim team. I taught you to drive and got you your car. And what do I get from you? Nothing but a pile of grief. Look at you! Everything about you says, 'Loser!' You've got no job, you're flunking out—you can't even keep your own room clean. All it is is your personal garbage dump!

"When I was your age I participated in sports, held two jobs, was an officer in my youth group, and had a 'B' average in school. I respected my parents, and you could walk through my room without stepping on yesterday's trash. I don't know what your problem is, but you better solve it quick or you're outta here! Sometimes I wonder where you came from! I just can't relate to who you are and what you do. Why don't you tell Paul what a good guy you are and how much you are mistreated at home?!"

I suppose that in the loosest sense of the word you could call this a confrontation or an exhortation. It certainly met the father's definition, but it doesn't meet God's. Is this your nightmare of confrontation? No wonder we all try to avoid something so cruel and unproductive! This kind of talk doesn't meet any of God's standards for communication, particularly in its message. What the father unwittingly communicated was this: "You are essentially different from me. You are a loser; I am a winner. You are irresponsible; I have always been responsible. I have hope; there is not much hope for you. I am righteous; you are tragically bound in sin, and judgment is coming soon."

I am sure that this is not what the father "officially" believed theologically. But in the heat of his struggle, he greeted the sinful, unbelieving, turning, hardening heart of his son with self-righteous, impatient condemnation. He did not offer him what he really needed: a humble, compassionate message of the grace of God for the struggle. Please understand: the grace of God *never* minimizes our sin, but it *does* give us a reason to face it, confess it, and forsake it. Grace is the only reason we have hope to continue our fight against sin. It is all we are called to offer others who blindly are beginning to turn away.

This father did not realize that he and his son were the same—not in the sense that they had committed identical sins and expressed identical attitudes, but in their need of the moment-by-moment grace of God. They were the same in the fact that thinking, speaking, and doing good were beyond their ability without the grace of God. They both needed to see God's hand at work in their daily lives. And they were the same in their need to follow him by faith, loving him above anything else.

But neither of them saw these things. They both sat there,

in their own ways tired, discouraged, doubting, rebellious, deceived, self-righteous, and confused. Dad thought, "I am a much better father than you are a son, and I have a right to give up on you." Joe, his son, thought, "I am a much better son than you are a father, and I have the right to give up on you." Both of them were self-deceived and ready to quit. Both needed a reason to continue. They needed someone to lovingly help them see their sins, just as King David once needed Nathan to do that for him. But they also needed to see the powerful presence of a loving Redeemer and his glorious grace at work in their lives. They needed to be compelled by his love, to stop living for themselves, and to start living for him. This is the everyday ministry of encouragement that should color our talk with one another. As we meet believers discouraged in the battle and blinded by sin, do we give them reason to hold on, to stay confident, and to continue the fight?

A Model of Biblical Confrontation

What could Joe's father have done differently? What are the elements of proper biblical confrontation? What must we do to avoid the pitfalls we've discussed in this chapter? To answer these questions let me present a model of confrontation that uses the word *ENCOURAGE* as an acrostic.

Examine your heart. Confrontation always begins with you. Because we all struggle with indwelling sin, we must begin with ourselves. We must be sure that we have dealt with our anger, impatience, self-righteousness, and bitterness. When we start with our own confession, we are in a much better place to lead another to confess.

Note your calling. Remember that confrontation is not based on your opinion of the person. You are there as an ambassador and your job is to faithfully represent the message of the King. In other words, your goal is to help people see and accept God's view of them.

Check your attitude. When you speak, are your words spoken in kindness, humility, gentleness, patience, forgiveness, forbearance, compassion, and love? Failure to do this will hinder God-honoring, change-producing confrontation. We need to examine both our message and our attitude as we speak.

Own your own faults. It is vital to enter moments of confrontation with a humble recognition of who we really are. As we admit our own need for the Lord's forgiveness, we are able to be patient and forgiving with the one to whom God has called us to minister.

Use words wisely. Effective confrontation demands preparation, particularly of our words. We need to ask God to help us use words that carry his message, not get in the way of it.

Reflect on Scripture. The content of confrontation is *always* the Bible. It guides what we say and how we say it. We should enter moments of confrontation with a specific understanding of what Scripture says about the issues at hand. This means more than citing proof texts; it means understanding how the themes, principles, perspectives, and commands of Scripture shape the way we think about the issues before us.

Always be prepared to listen. The best, most effective confrontation is interactive. We need to give the person an opportunity to talk, since we cannot look into his heart or read his mind. We need to welcome his questions and look for signs that he is seeing the things he needs to see. We need to listen for true confession and the commitment to specific acts of repentance. As we listen, we will learn where we are in the confrontation process.

Grant time for a response. We must give the Holy Spirit time to work. There is nothing in Scripture that promises that if we do our confrontation work well, the person will confess and repent in one sitting. Rather, the Bible teaches us that change is usually a process. We need to model the same patience God has granted us. This patience does not compromise God's work of change, but flows out of a commitment to it.

Encourage the person with the gospel. It is the awesome grace of God, his boundless love, and his ever-present help that give us a reason to turn from our sin. Scripture says that it is the kindness of God that leads people to repentance (Rom. 2:4). The truths of the gospel—both its challenge and its comfort— must color our confrontation.

Do you remember the tense and awkward scene between the man I counseled and his pastor and elders? How different their interaction would have been if the pastor had followed this model! Imagine how different the results would have been if Joe's father had approached him this way! Imagine the good that can result when confrontation is not a club, but a light, not a sentence of judgment but a loving call to change, not an announcement of hopelessness, but an encouragement to continue the fight with sin until the battle is finally won!

We all, in our own way, struggle with weariness, discouragement, doubt, rebellion, deception, self-righteousness, and confusion. We all need more than someone to point out all our sins! We need someone who will point us to Christ, reminding us of the confidence we once had in him and calling us back to a heart of faith. We need our blinders removed— not just the blinders that keep us from seeing our sin, but also the blinders that keep us from seeing Christ! Only in the light of his grace can we find a reason to confess and forsake sin. This is the encouragement we need every day.

Don't give up! There is reason to continue! Open your eyes to God's truth, open your heart to his conviction, open your life

to his grace, and follow him by faith. There is help and there
is hope!

> God is our refuge and strength,
>   an ever-present help in trouble.
> Therefore we will not fear, though the earth give way
>   and the mountains fall into the heart of the sea,
> though its waters roar and foam
>   and the mountains quake with their surging.
>   (Ps. 46:1–3)

Getting Personal: Examining Your Confrontation Style

1. Critique the last time you confronted someone
   (spouse, child, or friend) using the *ENCOURAGE*
   model as a guide. In what ways did you follow a biblical model? In what ways do you need to change the
   way you confront others?
2. Where have you avoided confrontation, leaving issues
   unresolved and relationships unreconciled?
3. Are you harboring anger or bitterness toward anyone
   that can hinder opportunities for constructive confrontation?
4. What sin has God recently shown you to remind you of
   your ongoing need of his grace? Does this keep you
   humble as you consider the failures of others?
5. What Scripture passages help you face your sin and
   continue your fight with it? What are your God-given
   opportunities to share these with others?

Chapter Ten

On the King's Mission

God has given us
the task of telling
everyone what
he is doing.
We're Christ's
representatives.
(2 Cor. 5:19–20)

AS he recounted it, I knew it was a story I wouldn't soon forget. It had all the ingredients of an ugly confrontation between a parent and an older child. There was the son's two-faced rebellion, a purposeful deception using his father's equipment to pull it off—all the typical stuff that sends parents over the edge. But this time things were different. The ugly scene didn't take place. More good than one would think possible resulted from something that started out looking terrible. What made the difference? Let me tell the story.

It was the end of an unusually busy day at work. Frank couldn't wait to get home, have a hot meal, and relax for a couple of hours before contacting some clients by e-mail later in the evening. As he drove home he muttered to himself, "I'm bushed!" But as he walked in the door, the smells of a great meal greeted him. He had time to read the paper before supper and a brief moment to relax afterwards. He was refreshed as he sat down at the computer in his home office. But when he checked the incoming e-mail, he was greeted with something that would completely alter his evening.

There was an e-mail for his son. He didn't usually read

Ryan's letters, but as he was printing it for him, Frank looked up and saw foul language in capital letters all over the computer screen. He stopped and read the letter. As he did, his heart sank. It was sexually disgusting, disrespectful, and hinted at events that, if true, made him wonder if he knew his own son.

He immediately began searching the computer for e-mails from Ryan to this friend. It wasn't long before he found the most recent letter. To his dismay, his son's letter was worse. It was so bad that Frank literally wept over its contents. He sat at the computer, stunned. "This filth was written by my son, who claims to be a committed Christian? How could he write this? How could he dare write it on the company computer? How could he put this trash out there for anyone to read?" The sadness quickly turned to anger. Red-faced, with e-mail in hand, he went to look for Ryan.

It was an act of God's grace that his son wasn't home. God had something good in mind for both of them. Frank called his wife, Ellen, to come into their bedroom. He stuck the e-mail in her face and said, "Take a look what our sweet little boy has been up to!" Like Frank, Ellen wept as she read what her son had written. "Where is he? I want to talk to him now!" Frank demanded, only to be told that Ryan was out studying. He would not be home until quite late. "I can't believe it! The one time we have to talk to him and he's not here!" Frank stormed. "Maybe it's for the best, dear. It will give us time to think," Ellen replied. Truer words have never been spoken.

As they began to talk, their perspective began to change. In a conversation that consumed most of the evening, Frank began to see the issue not so much as a personal affront but as an opportunity to minister to his son, who was clearly in the throes of great temptation and sin. Ellen was able to move beyond the goal of de-escalating Frank's anger to step back and take a more thoughtful look at the situation.

Together, they were impressed that God loved their son enough to expose his sin. The fact that Frank had needed to use the computer that evening, the fact that the e-mail "just happened" to come in from Ryan's friend, and the fact that Ryan was not home when things were uncovered were all part of God's plan of rescue. God the Redeemer had reached down to stop Ryan from continuing on the path he had begun. And God was calling Frank and Ellen to be part of what *he* was doing in Ryan's life at that moment.

This realization filled Frank and Ellen with joy and hope even in the midst of their hurt and sadness. These perspectives gave them a whole new set of things to say to Ryan, and a completely different way to say them. They imagined what the scene would have been had Ryan been home when Frank discovered the e-mails. Frank would have exploded in anger, Ryan would have exploded back or retreated into defensive silence, and none of the good that God had planned would have taken place.

The next morning Frank woke up and sat on the edge of the bed as he spoke to Ellen: "It hit me this morning, honey. None of this is about us. This is God's moment; we are just here as his instruments. I was thinking as I was lying here that Ryan really isn't ours. He belongs to God. God placed him in our hands so that we can be God's tools in his life. I'm hurt and I know you are too, but this is a wonderful opportunity to talk to Ryan about the most important things in life. Maybe this will sound funny, but it hit me that this is a *redemptive* moment. That's what God is doing in Ryan's life. He's working to rescue Ryan from sin and death, so he would not let Ryan be successful at his sin. He let it be exposed. God stuck it in our face, not so we would be depressed and discouraged, but so we would be his instruments of redemption in Ryan's life. It is so important that we handle this thing God's way! We can't let our hurt and anger get in the way of what God is doing. I am so glad we've had time to think and pray before we talked to Ryan."

They had their talk with Ryan that evening. And it didn't begin with Frank sticking the e-mail in Ryan's face and saying,

"How dare you do this to me, you sneaky little punk!" Rather, Frank started by asking Ryan if they could pray before they talked. Immediately Frank had Ryan's attention. He had never done this before! Frank then told Ryan what he had discovered. Then, very calmly, he told Ryan the two things he was feeling that night. The first was sadness at the thought of Ryan's deception and sin. The second was joy, because the whole situation pictured so clearly how much God loved Ryan and how actively he was working to rescue him from sin. He told Ryan that at the end of it all, he hoped Ryan would be overwhelmed with the love of God. It was a long conversation and a very late night, but a real turning took place in Ryan's heart that evening. And not only in Ryan's—there was a turning in Frank's heart as well.

When Frank later told me the story, he captured the change within himself very well. "For the first time, I began to think *redemptively* about the relationships around me. It hit me that if God was using this situation to do his work in Ryan, then he was doing the same in Ellen and our other children— and me. It's given me a whole new perspective on my family— and not just my family, but my friendships too. I realized that how I handle situations—what I say—is very important. Either I am taking control and handling things in the way that seems best to me, or I am responding in a way that makes me part of what God wants to do through the circumstance."

What a nice way to capture it! We all need a *redemptive perspective* on our relationships. Before we speak, we need to ask ourselves what the Redeemer wants to accomplish in the situation, and we need to be committed to be a part of it. We are meant to be on *his* mission. It is in the workroom of everyday life that God builds faithful, godly, and mature children, and we are the tools he uses. When Frank and Ellen got hold of this perspective, it completely transformed the way they dealt with their son's sin.

The lesson Frank learned is what this chapter is about. To speak as Christ's ambassadors, we must understand God's mission and how it offers us practical guidance for the things we face with family, friendships, and the body of Christ.

It's Been His Mission from the Beginning

From the first moments of sin's existence on the earth, God's response has been redemption. This is clear in his words to the Serpent after the Fall.

> So the LORD God said to the serpent, "Because you have done this,
>
> > "Cursed are you above all the livestock
> > and all the wild animals!
> > You will crawl on your belly
> > and you will eat dust
> > all the days of your life.
> > And I will put enmity
> > between you and the woman,
> > and between your offspring and hers;
> > he will crush your head,
> > and you will strike his heel." (Gen. 3:14–15)

In other words, God says to the Serpent, "I will not leave things as they are. Through the woman I will bring a Redeemer who will crush you and your work through his own suffering." God's response to Satan's lies and Adam and Eve's rebellion is not just to judge, but to redeem. Here God introduces the plan that unfolds throughout the rest of Scripture. The Bible is the story of God's work to redeem a people for himself, who will live forever to his glory. We are called to be part of this great work, which means that we must think about the events and people we encounter in a way that enfolds them (and us) in God's story of redemption. The only hope for *our* story is that we would be part of *his* story of redemption. The only right way to approach the events of our lives is to approach them redemptively.

This mission and our call to be part of it is clearly laid out in God's covenant call to Abram.

> *The LORD had said to Abram, "Leave your country, your people and your father's household and go to the land I will show you.*
>
> *"I will make you into a great nation*
> *and I will bless you;*
> *I will make your name great,*
> *and you will be a blessing.*
> *I will bless those who bless you,*
> *and whoever curses you I will curse;*
> *and all peoples on earth*
> *will be blessed through you." (Gen. 12:1–3)*

Volumes have been written about God's covenant with Abram, and my purpose here is not to add to that body of literature. But I want to make a very important observation about these words: they are both a *comfort* and a *call*. What greater comfort can there be than to be chosen as the object of God's blessing! But God never intended Abram to be *just* the object of his blessing. From Day One it was God's intention that Abram would also be the *conduit* of his blessing to others. Through Abram all the nations on earth would be blessed.

From the beginning, Abram was called to look beyond himself and to see his life redemptively. He was called to be part of what God was going to do not only *in* him and *for* him, but also *through* him. Here is the seed of every call to ministry found in the rest of Scripture. What happens throughout Scripture is that God waters and nurtures the seed of mission planted here until it is the fully mature tree of ministry revealed in the New Testament Epistles. What is clear in this covenant statement is that the God who is committed to redeem a people to himself has called his people to be committed to the same mission. We must never think of ourselves as *objects* of his covenantal love without also thinking of ourselves as *conduits* of that love to others.

Redemption is not just for our benefit or for our good. It has always been according to God's purpose and for his glory. We cannot treat salvation as a party where we are the honored guests. It is a celebration for a king to which we have been graciously (and amazingly) invited. What we celebrate is not just our invitation; we celebrate *him*, and we demonstrate our thanks by helping others come to know, serve, and celebrate him as well. It is *his* party! *He* is the guest of honor. All that we say and do should reflect a desire to be part of what he is doing, to bring him in some way the glory that is his due.

The Mission in Sharper Focus

Even as the Lord was giving his people the law in the Old Testament, he had this mission in view. The children of Israel were called to a radical commitment to God's redemptive work, which would lead to a radical involvement in each other's lives. They were called to speak in a way that promoted the work God was doing in the lives of others. Our part in the King's mission today could not be clearer than it is in Leviticus 19, a passage Christ alluded to when he summarized the law in Matthew 22.

> *Do not pervert justice; do not show partiality to the poor or favoritism to the great, but judge your neighbor fairly.*
> *Do not go about spreading slander among your people.*
> *Do not do anything that endangers your neighbor's life. I am the LORD.*
> *Do not hate your brother in your heart. Rebuke your neighbor frankly so you will not share in his guilt.*

Do not seek revenge or bear a grudge against one of your people, but love your neighbor as yourself. I am the LORD. (Lev. 19:15–18)

What does this passage say about our relationships? God is telling us that it is impossible for us to live as if sin doesn't exist. Because we are sinners and live in relationships with other sinners, sin will always be an issue. It is the inescapable reality of human life. The question is whether we are dealing with sin God's way (redemptively) or according to the desires and purposes of our own sinful hearts.

Love Your Neighbor as Yourself

Perhaps the first, most fundamental thing to notice in this passage is that the command to handle the sins of others God's way is directly connected to the command to love your neighbor as yourself. Loving your neighbors as yourself means many things, but of one thing we can be sure: it means dealing with their sin in a disciplined and distinctly biblical way. It means recognizing that we have been called by God to be part of what he is doing in their lives. We *are not* free to handle difficulties in whatever way seems best to us. When we are wronged, the thing of highest importance is not that we feel satisfied or avenged, but that we respond according to God's plan and for his glory.

As we recognize this calling, we do not give in to the many sins of heart and tongue that are detailed in this passage, even though they are such a temptation when we have been sinned against. Remember, we are dealing with the sins of others all the time. It will be this way until the Lord returns. Until then, loving your neighbor as yourself has this redemptive quality to it. It means that you deal with sin not simply as a victim, but as a servant of the One who redeems.

Let's face it: it is hard for us to love our neighbor as ourselves even when we haven't been sinned against! We are all prone to be self-centered, to want our will done our way, and to live for our own satisfaction and comfort. It's so easy to give in to irritation and impatience when in some way our will has not been done. I am not even referring to situations when we have encountered serious sin. No, we have trouble loving people who are only guilty of failing to please us!

Let me give you an example from my own life. One of the things I enjoy doing is going to bed at approximately the same time as Luella. She is my closest companion and my best friend, and I enjoy those final moments of warmth between us at the end of the day. Luella has a very melodic voice and I love having her voice be the last thing I hear before I go to sleep. These moments spent lying close to her and quietly talking are very precious.

One evening at about ten o'clock, I came up from our family room to head for bed, with the assumption that Luella would be heading in that direction as well. When I entered the kitchen, I couldn't believe what I saw! There was Luella, with a bucket and a brush, kneeling on the kitchen floor, getting ready to scrub it. Immediately I was filled with irritation. I couldn't believe she was doing this to me! Didn't she know that this was our special time? Did the floor have to be done *now*? It looked to me as if she was more committed to a clean floor than she was to her own husband.

Fortunately, I didn't say all the things I was thinking. But I did say, with an edge in my voice, "I can't believe you're doing this now!" as I went off to bed. I have thought about that scene many times since. What has hit me is not just my impatience, but the utter selfishness that lay behind it. As I looked at Luella, I did not see a loving and dedicated woman who also wanted to be in bed, but who had seen a job that needed to be done. I know what went through her head. That floor drives her crazy! With six people in the house, it always seems dirty. Here was an opportunity to get it done, because it was later in the evening and the kitchen traffic was light. Because of her loving dedication to her family, she seized the opportunity without grumble or complaint.

But as I looked at Luella that night, that is not what I saw. I saw a wife who was *supposed* to be heading to bed with me! There was no thanks to Luella or God in my heart. I went upstairs irritated that I had to go to bed alone because Luella had chosen the floor over me. Ridiculous? Embarrassing? Yes, but perhaps this is the power of this example. We struggle with the *little* events of life. We struggle to communicate in the midst of them in a godly way, even when we are *not* being sinned against. We lash out with angry, unkind words when the bathroom is occupied, or when the car is being used, or when someone else has beaten us to the remote control or the last donut, or when the newspaper is not there when we want to read it, or when someone is making us late, or when we don't get the appreciation we think we deserve, or when someone butts in line in front of us, or bumps us in a hallway, or forgets to leave the door unlocked, or neglects to put gas in the car, or stays too long on the phone . . . the list could go on and on!

This is where we live every day. If we respond selfishly to the normal give-and-take of relationships, how will we ever respond redemptively in the face of *real* sin? If we are not loving our neighbors in the normal course of things, how will we ever do it when the stakes are much, much higher? Again, we need to be gripped by the grandeur of our calling and the demands it makes on our daily talk. And we need to hold onto the truth that God has already given us everything we need to do what he has called us to do (2 Peter 1:3–4)!

How Will We Deal with Sin?

Since we are all affected by one another's sin in some way, we are all dealing with sin daily. The issue Leviticus puts before us is this: Are we dealing with it God's way or ours? Make no mistake, there is a stark contrast between the two.

Leviticus lays out for us the ways we can respond to the sin around us. In the center is the middle way of love, the road God has called us to travel in our relationships with one another. On either side are the valleys of hatred: on one side the passive forms of hatred and on the other the more active forms. We are commanded to stay on the middle road of love and not allow ourselves to fall off into either valley.

The valley of passive hatred includes inner attitudes of favoritism and partiality (Lev. 19:15), carrying hatred in your heart (v. 17), bearing a grudge (v. 18), and harboring desires of vengeance (v. 18). Clearly, none of these attitudes are consistent with God's call to love our neighbors as ourselves. Each reflects heart responses of self-love and anger against those who have not pleased us or satisfied our desires. Here our heart responses are shaped by our selfish expectations, not the glory of sharing in God's work on earth. There is no higher calling, yet it is one we easily forget in the press of life.

On the active side of hatred are things like treating people with favoritism and partiality (v. 15), judging others unfairly (v. 15), spreading slander (v. 16), and seeking revenge (v. 18). Again, these responses are the polar opposite of what God asks of us.

God does not want us to fall off the pathway of love on either side. Dwelling on someone's sin is an offense against God's calling to us. Desiring to see someone hurt the way we have been hurt is an offense against his calling. Keeping a record of wrongs is an offense against his calling. So is gossiping about someone's sin. Acting out any form of revenge is an offense against his calling. Yet if we examine our lives, we will find many of these responses present (see Matt. 18:15–19).

The wife who gives her husband the "silent treatment" when he has done something hurtful has responded vengefully and, in so doing, has forsaken her redemptive calling. The daughter who has been hurt by her parents and goes to her room, shuts the door, and recounts in graphic detail all the ways her family has failed her, has forsaken her calling.

The Christian brother who shares a juicy piece of gossip in the guise of a prayer request has fallen off the middle road of love and forsaken his calling. The husband who goes to work angry that his family made him late, who fantasizes how much easier life would be without them, has offended God's call.

How easy it is to fall off the road on either side! How hard and how high is God's call to love! Let's be humble and honest about our struggle to love one another in the way Leviticus depicts. Let's admit the many ways we fall off the pathway he has called for us to walk. Let's confess our shortcomings to God and each other, committing ourselves to specific acts of repentance.

The Middle Way of Love

The middle way of love is not about being nice or benignly tolerant of those we see doing wrong. Love is active! God wants us to be his agents of rescue when we see another's sin. He calls us to judge our neighbor fairly and to rebuke each other in a way that is frank and clear.

Having said this, please recognize that we are *not* told to be self-righteously judgmental, or to act like detectives, hunting for all the sin we can uncover in other people's lives. Nor are we called to be verbally abusive, coloring the confrontation with name-calling and other unkind characterizations. Rather, God is saying that when *he* chooses to expose another's sin to us, we are to respond with self-sacrificing, redemptive love. We go to our neighbor and honestly and clearly confront him with his sin—not so that he would submit to our judgments, but so that he would submit to God's and seek his mercy and grace. We want God, his will, and his mercy to loom large in the conversation—not us.

Something else is radical about this passage. It says that if we fail to do this, if we love ourselves more than we love God and others, if we allow ourselves to fall into those valleys of hatred, we will share in the guilt of our neighbor's sin! Yes, Cain, we are our brother's keeper (Gen. 4:9)! God's call could not be stronger. To fail to respond to another's sin with redemptive love is to share in his guilt. As God says through the prophet Ezekiel, if the watchman sees the enemy coming and fails to warn the people, their blood is on his hands (Ezek. 33:1–9). To be part of God's redemptive rescue is not only a high calling but a moral obligation.

We need the hearts of dedicated watchmen. The watchman's job is not to force people to respond to his warning; it is simply to give ample and timely warning. He is to make sure that his warning is understood and to entreat people to act upon it. Having done these things, his mission is complete. He has fulfilled his calling.

Our calling is to warn others to seek the protective, rescuing care of the Redeemer. Frank and Ellen didn't miss their calling. They entered Ryan's room as watchmen and their rebuke came as a loving warning that the Lord used to turn Ryan's heart. Everything they said flowed out of a heartfelt desire to be part of what God was doing. Don't miss the fact that before God could use their talk to work in Ryan's heart, he first had to work in theirs. And so it will be with us.

Finally, notice that this passage is punctuated twice with the words, "I am the LORD." God is saying, "This is the King speaking and this is *my* will for you. I am the LORD, and I am calling you to love one another this way. There is no room for debate or excuse or question. I am the LORD. Now go and be my instruments of warning and rescue to those I have placed near you."

The Great Commission

One of the clearest calls to be part of the King's mission on earth is found in Matthew 28. After the resurrection, Christ asked his disciples to meet him on a mountain in Galilee.

Here he spoke words of commission with which every believer is familiar, yet I wonder if Frank and Ellen would have thought that this commission applied to what they were doing with Ryan. I wonder if we see its application to *our* daily relationships. I am persuaded that these words have lost much of their power because of the way they are typically interpreted.

Consider Christ's great mission call to his disciples and his church, and ask yourself, What is this ministry? What impact does it have on our daily conversations? What demands does it make on the world of talk?

> *Then the eleven disciples went to Galilee, to the mountain where Jesus had told them to go. When they saw him, they worshiped him; but some doubted. Then Jesus came to them and said, "All authority in heaven and on earth has been given to me. Therefore go and make disciples of all nations, baptizing them in the name of the Father and of the Son and of the Holy Spirit, and teaching them to obey everything I have commanded you. And surely I am with you always, to the very end of the age." (Matt. 28:16–20)*

Christ stands before his disciples as the conquering King. Having completed his mission on earth and soon to be seated at the right hand of the Father, he lays claim to his authority and calls his followers to take his message to all the nations of the earth. We have all heard gripping appeals to be part of world missions based on this passage. Those appeals are appropriate and needed. But please notice that if we only interpret the passage this way, it leaves most of the church of Jesus Christ without a commission! That simply does not do justice to what is recorded here.

When God's people limit this passage to the world of foreign missions, they miss much of its meaning. The same thing happens when we limit the passage to a career ministry context. It becomes a passage about the full-time, career, foreign missionary who has accepted the call of the Great Commission! Certainly this passage *includes* these applications, but there is more here as well.

I believe that the church has been weakened by its tendency to neglect the second half of this commission. Jesus calls us not only to go and make disciples, but also to teach them what it means to live lives that are obedient to every command of Christ. It is a call to exhort, encourage, and teach so that we would be progressively freed from old patterns of sin and conformed instead to the image of Christ. The Great Commission is not only a call to bring people *into* the kingdom of light, but also a call to teach them to *live* as children of light once they are there. When we lose sight of this second half of the Great Commission ("teaching them to obey everything I have commanded you"), we lose sight of its claim on our everyday talk.

The Great Commission as a Lifestyle

Now, it is important to ask whose ministry this is and when and where it will be carried out. The answer all over the New Testament is that this is the ministry of every believer, to be done wherever and whenever needed. It is not only a call to a career of ministry, but more fundamentally to a *lifestyle* of ministry. This commission keeps us from divorcing ministry from our normal, everyday lives. Where do we teach and learn to live as obedient children of God? Not just in the formal programs of the church, but in everyday life experiences, where we wrestle with the temptations of the enemy and the desires of the sinful nature. So the husband and wife relationship becomes a forum for Great Commission ministry. The parent-child relationship becomes a forum for Great Commission ministry. Relationships in the body of Christ become a forum for Great Commission ministry, a commission that is not only about justification, but about progressive sanctification as well.

This means that when I want to talk with my wife about difficulties and disappointments in our relationship, I do so with a "second-half of the Great Commission" mentality. I acknowledge that the most important goal of the conversation is that our words encourage the work God is doing in both of us. The very fact that we need to talk indicates that this work is not yet complete. Even minor offenses reveal that we are not yet obeying all of Christ's commands. So, as we seek to understand each other and solve problems together, we want to promote the work God is doing to help us live more fully as children of light. Again, the issue is not *whether* we deal with the problems, but *how*. Is our approach shaped by a desire to minister his truth to each other until that ministry is no longer needed?

A "life is ministry" attitude must govern all the words we speak. We do not step *out* of life *into* ministry. God's call extends to every moment of life! Our response is to submit to the moral obligation to love our neighbors as ourselves, motivated by more than our own happiness, satisfaction, and comfort. We want to be part of what the King is doing in the lives of those around us.

These opportunities may not look like what we expect. Rarely will someone say, "What does the Bible say about . . . ?" or "I have recognized areas of my life that are out of conformity to God's will and I need your help." Or "Dad, are there a few more commands of Scripture that I need to apply to my life?" No, the most powerful moments of ministry come in times of difficulty, large and small. We know that the Lord uses difficulty to advance his work in our lives. And if we are one of his primary instruments of change, most likely some of our most wonderful ministry opportunities will come in moments we would rather avoid.

Often in such moments we are so caught up in our own emotions (hurt, fear, disappointment, anger, embarrassment, discouragement, etc.) or so caught up in our own desires (for a quick solution, to be right, to be appreciated, to escape, to win, to get out with the least amount of damage, for comfort and understanding, etc.) that we lose sight of the opportunity God has given us to speak words that promote his redemptive mission. When Frank first read Ryan's e-mail, he didn't think, *What a wonderful opportunity for ministry! Thank you, Lord!* No, his heart was filled with a father's grief, and that is appropriate. But those painful words, written in black and white in a way Ryan could not deny, were what God used to mobilize Frank and Ellen and to rescue Ryan. That moment of grief was not Frank and Ellen's moment, it was God's. He exposed them to things in Ryan's heart that he already knew were there. He called them to share in the suffering so that they would share in the glory of his work of change.

Frank and Ellen needed to get beyond the talk that is driven by racing emotions and fearful desire. ("How could you do this to us?" "We do and do for you and this is the thanks we get?" "That e-mail just proves you are in the right company— a loser hanging around with losers!" "Don't think that you are ever going to use that computer again! You have lost it for life!" "It's hard to believe that you are my son. Why, in my day I wouldn't have thought of doing such a thing!" "For once, we would just like you to do something we could respect!") They had to speak to Ryan out of the redemptive love of God. That love was the reason for this opportunity. It enabled them to reject arrogant, self-righteous words and offer instead humble words of grace. They approached Ryan as sinners who had experienced the intervening hand of the Redeemer themselves, and who longed for him to experience the same powerful, delivering grace.

A rebuke is not a condemnation but a call. Words of exhortation are not a judgment, but an encouragement to follow the Lord. The confrontation is not a sentence, but a warning. We speak God's words to each other not because we are higher or better and not because we are capable of fixing people. No, we teach, encourage, admonish, correct, and exhort because God has commissioned us to do so. This call is not one sector of our already-too-busy lives; it is itself a lifestyle. It is what we are to be doing wherever we are, whoever we are with.

Ministry will come unexpectedly, often wrapped in difficulty. In the midst of these opportunities, we want our talk to be consistent with God's call, for we have accepted the fact that we have been chosen to be on the King's mission.

Getting Personal: Whose Mission, Yours or the King's?

1. How do you typically respond to trouble? (Engage in self-pity? Question God? Blame others? Curse situations? Look for God's hand? Seek to serve?)
2. Where do you tend to turn moments of ministry into moments of frustration, irritation, and anger?
3. What does it mean to view relationships redemptively? Do you have any relationships that you fail to see this way?
4. Has fear caused you to trim the truth, avoid issues, or excuse someone's sin rather than confront him?
5. Where have you tended to personalize things that are not personal and in so doing miss God-given opportunities to speak redemptively?
6. What difficulty in your life is giving you an opportunity to do Great Commission work?
7. In your relationships, when do you tend to forget the promises of the gospel and become overwhelmed by God-given opportunities?
8. Confess any sins you've uncovered through these questions to God and the appropriate people. Embrace the promise of 1 John 1:8–9.

(part three)

winning the war of words

The right word at the right time
is like a custom-made piece of jewelry. . . .
(Prov. 25:11)

Lord, today there may be someone
who needs me
as an arm to lift life's load,
an eye to lead the lost,
a mind to learn Love's law.
May my arm not be slack,
my eye not grow dim
nor my mind fail to comprehend.
Rather, make me strong,
give me discernment,
fill me with truth.
Lord, I don't want to be
unprepared, unsteady, unsure
when his need is made known.
So, help me and use me
to bless my neighbor
according to Your will
and in
Your name,
Amen.

Chapter Eleven

First Things First

The health of
the apple tells
the health of the
tree. . . .Your true
being brims over
into true words
and deeds.
(Luke 6:45–46)

AS you get near the end of this book, perhaps you're thinking, *Paul, I understand God's
call regarding my words. I know I have not spoken
redemptively. My words have been driven by my
own desires, and I can see the fruit of my sin and
failure all over. But I don't know what to do!*

This chapter is for you. It is a chapter about
turning. We want to look at God's way of repentance. As you turn from the old way of talking, it is important to get first things first and
start with your heart. Repentance in Scripture is defined as a radical change *in your heart* that leads to a radical change *in your life.*
When God called Israel to repent he said, "Rend your heart and
not your garments. Return to the LORD your God" (Joel 2:13).
Tearing your garments was a symbol of remorse in Old Testament
culture, so God was essentially saying, "I want more than symbolic
acts of repentance. I want hearts that are truly changed."

The Foundation of Repentance:
Hearts that Embrace the Gospel

It is hard to understand but true nonetheless that God
shows us our sin and failure not as an act of condemnation,

but as an act of redeeming love. As a Father he disciplines his children *for the purpose of making us holy*. His intent is never to crush, destroy, or forsake. Though discipline can be painful, its purpose is to produce in us a harvest of righteousness and peace (Heb. 12:1–13).

So don't give in to despair. Don't let the enemy trick you into thinking that it is too late or that you will never get it right. Don't let your sense of failure cause you to turn from the Lord in guilt and shame. Turn *to* him and see in his face the loving acceptance of a father, a father who forces you to see yourself as you really are *because* he loves you deeply and fully.

Perhaps your eyes have been opened through this book, and you have seen things about your communication that you had not seen before. Come to the Lord in your brokenness. Seek his forgiveness and help. If God has convicted you, this can be either a moment of turning or a moment of hardening. Be encouraged and repent! You are loved!

True repentance begins with a heart that rests in the work of Christ and the many promises that flow out of his victory over sin. I want to highlight six of these promises because they are what encourage me to come out of the darkness into the searching light of truth. Sin produces guilt, shame, and fear, but only the Lord's perfect love drives it all away. In his great and precious promises I really do find everything I need to do what he has called me to do (2 Peter 1:3–4).

The first gospel promise we need to embrace is the promise of *forgiveness*. God's promise of forgiveness is full and complete. He says that he will remember our sins no more, but will separate us from those sins as far as the east is from the west! What an awesome promise! I do not have to carry my sins around like a huge duffel bag of regret that bruises my spiritual shoulders and breaks the back of my faith. Jesus took the weight of my sin on himself so that I would not have to carry it any longer.

What freedom is found here! It makes no sense for a believer to live imprisoned by fear, in the darkness of guilt and shame. Jesus has paid the debt! So, though I come stained and dirty, I can come to Christ full of faith and hope, and receive the forgiveness that is mine as a child of God.

The second promise of the gospel is *deliverance*. Christ came not only to forgive our sins, but to deliver us from them. On the cross he broke the power of sin's mastery over me (see Rom. 6:1–14). I do not have to give in any longer to sins of the tongue. Things *can* be different. I *can* speak in a new way.

In the gospel I find not only forgiveness and deliverance, but also *strength*. As the Lord promised Paul, "My grace is sufficient for you, for my power is made perfect in weakness" (2 Cor. 12:9). Yes, we fall short of God's standard. In ourselves we can do no good thing. But the Lord has not left us there. He comes in his power and fills us with his Spirit so that we can speak in a way that benefits others and glorifies him. The same power that raised Christ from the dead is living within us (Eph. 1:19–20). So we no longer have to succumb to weakness. We can speak out of the strength that is ours in Christ.

Another precious promise of the gospel is *restoration*. It is so easy to look back on our lives and see the wreckage of lost opportunity. It is so tempting to wish we could take words back and say what is right this time. It is so easy to question why God took so long to show us how far our words have fallen short.

Here the Lord's promise of restoration is so sweet. "I will repay you for the years the locusts have eaten. . . . You will have plenty to eat, until you are full, and you will praise the name of the LORD your God" (Joel 2:25–26). God is a Restorer. The years have not been wasted. In his sovereign love, God has been bringing us to this point of insight and conviction at just the right moment. His timing is always right. The process has been tailor-made to accomplish what he promised—a harvest of righteousness. And wonderfully, God promises to restore what has been lost in the process so that we, his people, will not be put to shame (Joel 2:27)!

In the gospel we also find the promise of *reconciliation*. The heart of the gospel is the coming of the Prince of Peace. In

him we find reconciliation not only with God, but with one another. He is the only One who can destroy the walls that separate people (Eph. 2:14–18). He alone is able to put love in
hearts where hate once reigned. He makes thoughtless, self-
absorbed people tender and compassionate. Out of the coal
of human sin and failure he produces the jewel of godliness.
He came so that the hearts of fathers would be turned once
again to their children and the hearts of children to their fathers (Mal. 4:6). He came so that his church would be a community of unity and love (John 17:20–23). He came so that
husbands and wives would live as one flesh. So there is hope
that where relationships have been damaged or even destroyed, real healing and reconciliation can take place. Your
Savior is the Prince of Peace!

Further, the gospel brings the promise of *wisdom*. James
talks about this almost matter-of-factly: "If any of you lacks wisdom, he should ask God" (James 1:5). How simple, yet how
encouraging! You may be thinking, *I know I need to change in
my communication, but I don't know where to start or what to do!*
What you need is wisdom, and not only does God give wisdom,
but he gives it *generously* and *without finding fault*. We have no
reason to despair over our own ignorance when "all the treasures of wisdom and knowledge" are hidden in Christ (Col.
2:3). His invitation is simple: "Come, ask, and I will give!"

Finally, the gospel promises us *mercy*. The writer of Hebrews reminds us that Jesus was tempted like we are in every
point, so he understands and sympathizes with our weaknesses. We can come to him and find mercy and grace to help
us in our time of need (Heb. 4:14–16). In the hardest of situations, in the most trying of relationships, we never stand alone
with only our personal abilities to help us. We are in Christ,
and in him we can do what would otherwise be impossible.

I cannot love my enemies. I cannot do good to those who
mistreat me. I cannot be patient in the face of provocation. I
cannot honor when I am dishonored. I cannot leave
vengeance to the Lord. I cannot find delight in self-sacrificing

service. I cannot speak softly in the face of another's anger. I am not naturally kind, compassionate, gentle, or forgiving. The standard is too high and the calling is too great for me to fulfill. But that is why Jesus came. In him we really do find *everything* we need!

The gospel is the soil in which real repentance grows. Its promises make me willing to face my sin and give me the strength to turn from it. Real hope for real change is found in Christ! Repentance is built on that foundation.

The next question is, What does true repentance look like? How would a real change of heart be revealed in your communication? This leads us to consider the steps of true repentance, the kind of heart change that leads to life change.

Consideration:
The First Step of Repentance

The first step in the repentance process is to confess that we tend to be spiritually blind. We see others' sin and failure much more clearly than we do our own. We all too readily make excuses and shift the blame, leaving ourselves with a distorted picture of who we are and what we have done.

The remedy is quite simple. We need to look intently in the mirror of God's Word to see ourselves as we really are, and to see where change needs to take place (James 1:22–25). As we look into God's mirror we need to ask, What does God want to show me that I haven't yet seen about my life of talk?

As we read Scripture, we will see that the Bible's emphasis on communication is not so much a focus on new techniques as it is a heart agenda that turns talk from an untameable world of evil to a grace-giving world of good. Out of this agenda flow practical biblical principles of communication that define what it means to *speak redemptively*. No longer will our words leave a trail of discouragement, destruction, and division. Rather, they will be words of love, truth, grace, hope, faith, forgiveness, and peace, producing a harvest of right-eousness.

The Heart Behind the Struggle

A couple I counseled several years ago illustrates our desperate need to *consider* the hearts that control our words. I had been counseling Bob and Mary for a while. One of Bob's consistent struggles with Mary was the frequency and intensity of her anger toward their three children. I had encouraged Bob not just to complain to me about Mary's anger, but to commit himself to speaking the truth to Mary.

The three of us had gotten together again and Bob was summarizing the events of the week. "Oh, by the way," he said, "I took your advice and confronted Mary about her anger. I told her she needed to examine how destructive it is and the way it interferes with what God wants to do in the lives of our kids." As I listened to Bob, I had two conflicting reactions. The first was that what Bob communicated sounded right and good. The second reaction came from watching Mary as Bob talked. She was not buying his summary at all. In fact, she was clearly angry at how good the summary made Bob look!

I said, "Mary, you seem upset by what Bob has said. Why don't you tell me what you're thinking?" Mary described the scene this way. "I had decided to make us all a good home-cooked meal for a change. It's been so hard with a five-year-old and three-year-old twins. The afternoon was unbelievable. The boys seemed like they had plotted to do anything they could to keep me from getting a decent meal on the table. I did manage to make dinner, but by the time we sat down to eat, I was totally frazzled. As usual the meal began with one of the twins spilling his drink all over everything. Well, I lost it. I not only yelled at him, but at the other two for thinking it was so funny.

"At this point I looked up at Bob and I could tell he was really steaming. At first he just sat there glaring at me. Then he began to speak, right in front of the kids. He said, 'When are you ever going to learn? Are you so full of yourself and your little problems that you can't see what's happening? Are you totally blind to what you have become? You are the single most destructive thing in our children's lives. I wonder if they will ever recover from what you have done to them. Sometimes I wonder if it would have been better if they had never met you! And I have given up any hope of you changing! Sure, you say you're sorry, but you turn right around and do it all over again. You need to get your act together or get away from the kids! You've never heard *me* lash out in anger against them like you do. I just wish that you could look at yourself and see what I see!' I looked around the table and saw all three of our boys listening intently as Bob tore me apart."

There is much that could be said about this family's struggles, but for our purposes here I want to focus on Bob in his role as God's spokesman. As husband, father, and believer, he has been called by God to be an ambassador. He has been called to be a watchman. He has been called to encourage perseverance and to be an agent of rescue and restoration. Mary was in the midst of a very significant spiritual struggle. She was blind to herself and God's presence and power. Clearly, she needed help, and clearly Bob had been positioned to be God's helper in Mary's life. Yet when Bob looked at Mary, this is not what he saw. He saw someone who was messing up his otherwise orderly life. He saw someone he wanted to be free from, rather than a loved one in need of rescue. What Bob said was neither helpful nor productive. His words did not produce a harvest of righteousness. They only made Mary more defensive. Instead of opening her spiritual eyes, Bob's words only aggravated her blindness.

You could argue, in a loose sense, that what Bob said is true. Mary's anger *is* harmful to the children. She *is* blind to what she is doing. She *does* confess, but there is no lasting repentance. Yet the truth of Bob's words is so distorted by his own sinful attitudes that what he says ceases to be the truth.

Instead we hear the angry opinion of a man who is just as blind as Mary. Bob neglected to put first things first. He didn't take time to deal with his own heart attitudes, so his words didn't offer solutions and comfort. Instead they became another part of the problem.

Imagine the difference if Bob hadn't blurted out his words at the table that night. Imagine if he had waited, taking time to grapple with the war in his own heart. Imagine if he had confessed his anger against Mary and began to focus on what God wanted to accomplish. Imagine if he had seen the moment as *God's* moment of redemption and restoration. What a difference there would have been if he had spoken truth with patience, gentleness, humility, and love!

Mary didn't look back with thankfulness for the way God used Bob in her life. She wasn't testifying to his loving frankness. Instead she was angry with Bob for the "horrible" things he said. She was outraged at how and where he said them. Mary's eyes were fixed on Bob, just as Bob's had been on Mary. There was no redemptive change taking place; the problem had just added another layer of complication.

Take time to look at yourself in the mirror of God's Word. Have you spoken to others without first examining your own heart? Have your words brought hope, help, and comfort to those struggling with sin? Or has your communication only added layers of difficulty to the mound already there? Take time to consider the gentle voice of the Redeemer as he speaks to you through his Word.

Confession: The Second Step of Repentance

Real repentance always involves confession. We accept responsibility before God and man for what we have said and done. Confession means humbly accepting what God has said about us—that we are sinners by nature and our sin is expressed in our thoughts, words, and actions. We cannot confess sins of communication without confessing the sinful attitudes that have shaped our words. This is where the story of Bob and Mary can help us. What heart attitudes lay beneath Bob's words to Mary? Remember, Mary wasn't the only one in the midst of a spiritual battle; Bob was as well. Remember also that the war of words always reveals a deeper war. Bob and Mary were both up against an enemy who would like to divide and destroy their whole family. He was encouraging several attitudes in Bob's heart. Do you need to confess these attitudes as well?

1. *Doubt.* Mary's anger was the occasion for much doubt in Bob. First, he wondered if he had been "totally out of God's will" when he married Mary. Had he been so taken with her physical beauty that he failed to take time to get to know her? He also doubted God. He said, "I just don't understand why God would let me marry such a person. Nothing has shaken my belief in God's wisdom more than my marriage."

2. *Fear.* Bob expressed it this way: "I look at our children and wonder what kind of monsters they will grow up to be. I can see them someday talking with a counselor about how awful their home was. It feels like every room I go into, there is Mary and she is upset about something. Most of the time I try not to think about where all of this is leading."

3. *Anger.* "I don't want much," Bob said. "I just want a home with a little bit of order and love. Is that too much to ask? I'm doing my part; all I'm asking is that Mary do hers."

4. *Vengeance.* It seemed to Bob as if Mary could sin day after day and nothing would happen. "Why does God let this go on?" Bob wondered. "Why doesn't he do something? I would like Mary to hurt just once the way she hurts the children and me."

5. *Self-righteousness.* "I just don't understand Mary's anger. I guess we are just different. I have never felt the anger that Mary feels, let alone expressed it! I would never think of saying the cruel things she says to the boys. Sometimes I wonder if she is even a Christian. If she is, I can't relate to her brand of Christianity!"

6. *Selfishness.* "A man needs a place to retreat. I've got nowhere. When I punch out at night, I want the tough part of my day to be over. I don't want a home more stressful than my work. I shouldn't have to be on the job twenty-four hours a day. When do I get time off?"

7. *Hopelessness.* Bob felt trapped and completely powerless to effect change. He said, "The way I see it, I can't change Mary yet I am forced by God to stay with her. If I stay, I lose because my life gets swallowed up in her anger. If I leave, I lose because I will face God's judgment. I pray about this every day, but God just doesn't seem to be listening. I go to church and I see all of those happy families sitting together and I get sick to my stomach. I'm trapped and I don't know what to do!"

It is tempting here to respond to each of Bob's attitudes, but I do not want to lose sight of the main point we are considering: There is no way that Bob will speak redemptively—no way he will function as God's ambassador and watchman—without first dealing with the war going on in his own heart, the war his words reveal. Bob saw the war going on in Mary, and he recognized how it shaped her communication. Yet he failed to recognize the same war within himself and the way *that* war shaped his words to Mary.

Bob not only missed an opportunity to be part of what God was doing in Mary's life, but his behavior made things worse. Mary grew more and more defensive, more and more unwilling to listen to Bob. She focused more and more on

Bob's sin and not on her own. Bob hadn't been used of God to lift her blindness; he had been the tool of the enemy to intensify it. Why? Because he had failed to deal with first things first and face his own heart issues. Thus he was unprepared to "speak the truth in love."

Commitment:
The Third Step of Repentance

We all tend to share Bob's struggle. We are prone to speak without proper heart preparation. And so we need to commit ourselves to start first with our own hearts. James says that we should be slow to speak (James 1:19–21). Proverbs says that the heart of a righteous man weighs his answer (Prov. 15:28). But we are inclined to rehearse the sins of others rather than to examine our own hearts. When we give in to these tendencies, we become part of the problem rather than instruments of change.

Nowhere is there a clearer call to heart preparation than in the words of Paul to the Colossian church.

> *Therefore as God's chosen people, holy and dearly loved, clothe yourselves with compassion, kindness, humility, gentleness and patience. Bear with each other and forgive whatever grievances you may have against one another. Forgive as the Lord forgave you. And over all these virtues put on love, which binds them all together in perfect unity.*
>
> *Let the peace of Christ rule in your hearts, since as members of one body you were called to peace. And be thankful. Let the word of Christ dwell in you richly as you teach and admonish one another with all wisdom, and as you sing psalms, hymns and spiritual songs with gratitude in your hearts to God. And whatever you do, whether in word or deed, do it all in the name of the Lord Jesus, giving thanks to God the Father through him. (Col. 3:12–17)*

This passage is one of the Bible's most direct calls to personal ministry. Paul calls us to do things with one another that are often assigned to the realm of professional, formal ministry. Paul calls each of us to be teachers. He calls each of us to be admonishers. He calls all of us to sing the truth to one another. We are all to take advantage of the unique opportunities God gives us to be part of what he, as Redeemer, is doing. But as striking as this call is to personal ministry, most of the passage is not about what we have been called to do. Most of it is about *preparing* for it, about the posture of heart that makes ministry possible.

All of us are people of influence. All of us are trying to make sense out of life and sharing our interpretations with others. This world of influence and "ministry" is unavoidable. The giving and receiving of counsel is the stuff of human relationships. The question is this: Are we *committed* to this ministry, and to doing it God's way? Are we willing to function as his ambassadors? Are we preparing ourselves so that he *can* make his appeal through us?

In verse 12, as Paul describes the heart preparedness needed for personal ministry, he uses a common metaphor we do not want to miss. Paul says that we should "clothe" ourselves with certain attitudes. He is essentially saying, "If you are going to minister to one another, you'd better get dressed for the job! Here is the heart clothing God provides so that you can speak redemptively."

1. *Compassion*: Compassion is not only a deep awareness of another's need; it is a desire to do something to relieve it. We are the children of One who is "the Father of compassion and the God of all comfort, who comforts us in all our troubles, so that we can comfort those in any trouble with the comfort we ourselves have received from God" (2 Cor. 1:3–4). It makes no sense to receive such amazing compassion and respond to others harshly and unsympathetically.

2. *Kindness.* To be kind is to be generous, tender, and warm-hearted. It means to speak and act in a way that is understanding and considerate. Yet isn't it true that too often in marriage, parenting, and the church, times of admonishment lack tenderness? Ask yourself, when you confront, exhort, admonish, or teach, does a warm and considerate spirit characterize these times?

3. *Humility.* Often, times of personal ministry lack a "standing-alongside" spirit. Yet we *are* fundamentally like those to whom we minister. If I am a parent, for example, there is no sin my child would commit that hasn't been present in my life in some way. We *do* stand right next to those we serve as people in moment-by-moment need of the forgiving, delivering, and enabling grace of the Lord. Humility simply means that we bring a biblically accurate self-assessment to the Lord's work. This will lead us to speak out of a humble sense of a shared need for Christ (see Heb. 2:10–18 and the example of Christ).

4. *Gentleness.* When my son Darnay was about three years old, he picked some flowers for his mom. At least we think they were flowers! By the time the "bouquet" reached the house, the stems were twisted, bent, and limp, the blossoms crushed and torn. Luella decided that the only way to display the flowers was to float the few blossoms that weren't hopelessly damaged in a shallow crystal dish. There was nothing wrong with what Darnay tried to do. His problem was that he lacked gentleness. Fortunately, Luella's gentle, gracious response made up for it.

Gentleness treats others with tenderness, speaking in a way that is soft and mild. Proverbs tells us that harsh words create problems rather than solve them (Prov. 15:1). Gentleness means that I don't damage the very person I am seeking to help. Gentleness doesn't mean compromising the truth. Rather, it means keeping the truth from being compromised by harshness and insensitivity.

5. *Patience.* One of the hardest things God calls us to in our relationship with him and with others is to wait. We do not like to wait for the harvest. We want to plant seeds in the morning and harvest mature fruit in the afternoon. But God's work of change, in us and in others, is a process.

We want change to be an event, so we speak in haste and apply human pressure in the forms of guilt and ultimatums. We thus complicate problems, and whatever solutions we enjoy prove to be temporary and cosmetic. Patience is being willing to wait even when that means enduring difficulty. And patience means not only waiting, but waiting *calmly.* Impatience is revealed by the anger that grows with each minute. Patience waits without giving in to impulsive words or actions.

6. *Forbearance.* Forbearance is patience under pressure. The hardest time to exercise patience is when we are being provoked. Forbearance means refraining from retaliation, holding back in the face of provocation. Peter says this of Christ: "When they hurled their insults at him, he did not retaliate; when he suffered, he made no threats. Instead, he entrusted himself to him who judges justly" (1 Peter 2:23). What an example! Notice that Christ's forbearance grew in the soil of an active trust in the justice of the Father.

7. *Forgiveness.* When I have been sinned against, I must renounce my feelings of anger and bitterness and my desire for vengeance. This prepares me to forgive when the person confesses the sin and asks for forgiveness. In this face-to-face encounter, I free the person from the fault and from any need for payment. As sinners, we dare not receive the forgiveness of others while we ourselves struggle to forgive. (See the parable of the unmerciful servant, Matt. 18:21–35.)

8. *Love.* This is the ultimate quality, the virtue that holds all the others together. It is the fundamental ingredient of redemption, and it must be the fundamental character of our

ministry to one another. Love means the willingness to sacrifice personal position, possessions, desires, and needs for the good of another. It is a willingness to wait, work, suffer, and give for the benefit of another. Love means being willing to lay down my life for another.

9. *Peace.* Peace is not an absence of conflict or strife, but a position of heart that shapes ministry. The peace to which we are called is the peace *of Christ.* This is what must rule our hearts rather than the situational and relational "what ifs" that so often control us.

Often when parents discover that their teenager has lied to them, gone somewhere forbidden, or skipped school, they let their minds run wild, conceiving every possible worst case scenario. (What else are they doing that I don't know about? Are there drugs involved? What other lies have they been telling me? How often have they missed school?) Rather than recognizing that the uncovering of their child's sin is the result of God's presence and love, their words are shaped by fear, come across as accusations, and do not lead to the change needed. The mistake was to let communication flow from the fear of circumstances rather than the peace of Christ.

Peace is an inner rest, contentment, security, and hope that stems from an active trust in the presence, power, rule, and grace of Christ. It is a habit of daily rest in Christ. It comes from looking at life from the vantage point of who God is and what he is doing as Lord and Redeemer.

10. *Thankfulness.* We live in an age of rights and entitlement, an age of "I deserve. . . ." On the street it's called "props," that is, the *proper* recognition that everyone "deserves." But if we remember what the gospel says about who we are and what we really deserve, it should not be difficult to live and speak out of a thankful heart! Thankfulness is a spirit of gratitude for gifts and graces that we could not achieve or

earn. It reflects an awareness of the incredible mercy I continue to receive from the Lord's hand. I am called to speak out of this kind of heart.

These character qualities are the "clothing" we are to put on as God's instruments of redemption. There are two things to say about this list. First, we must humbly confess that we fall far short of the standard held out here. It simply is not humanly achievable! We must cry out for the mercy and strength of God, who is at work within us even as we pray.

Second, it is vital to understand what Paul is actually telling us to "wear." He is saying, "Put on *Christ*!" This is what this list is about—Christ. Paul is saying, "Take on the character of Christ as you speak to one another. Incarnate Christ in your ministries in the same way that he incarnated the Father on earth. Bring the glory of Christ with you as you minister. He is your only hope of change. Confront one another not just with human words, human wisdom, and human arguments. Confront one another with the presence and glory of Christ. Reinforce the reality that he is here and active. Be a window to his glory!"

This means letting go of any hope that *we* can produce change. You and I *don't* produce change in others; it is always the result of God's power and grace at work. So we let go of human demands. We don't try to impress people with how much we know or how much we've experienced. We don't try to force change by manipulation. We don't seek to get results with a loud voice or inflammatory words. We won't bribe, bargain, or make deals. We won't seek to get responses by guilt, condemnation, or judgment. We don't trust in our airtight arguments. We recognize that if these things could bring lasting change to the human heart, Christ would never have come to suffer and die. The most important encounter in personal ministry is not people's encounter with us, but their encounter with him. We are simply called to set up that encounter.

So we prepare ourselves for personal ministry by clothing

ourselves with Christ and coming armed with the truths of Scripture. When these things are in place, we are ready to speak redemptively.

Change: The Final Step of Repentance

There is a simple repentance principle that must be remembered: Change has not taken place until change has taken place. Repentance is a change of heart that leads to a radical change in your life, in its relationships and daily situations. Since it is out of the heart that the mouth speaks, heart change will always lead to communication change. A heart submitted to Christ will produce Christlike talk. Repentance is not only about saying no to ungodliness, but also about living self-controlled, upright, and godly lives. Repentance always involves "put off" *and* "put on" (Eph. 4:22–24).

What causes a person to pursue the character of Christ? What makes us long to be conformed to his image? As I have counseled many struggling husbands and wives, I have been impressed by how many of them have a firm grasp on Scripture's teaching about marriage, but have serious marital problems because they lack the character of Christ. Their biblical knowledge doesn't serve them well because their hearts aren't conformed to Christ. In fact, in many of these relationships, biblical knowledge is used as a weapon in the marital war. Why are Christlike attitudes missing in people who profess to be believers and are active in their local church?

Peter addresses this issue in his second letter:

> *His divine power has given us everything we need for life and godliness through our knowledge of him who called us by his own glory and goodness. Through these he has given us his very great and precious promises, so that through them you may participate in the divine nature and escape the corruption in the world caused by evil desires.*

For this very reason, make every effort to add to your faith goodness; and to goodness, knowledge; and to knowledge, self-control; and to self-control, perseverance; and to perseverance, godliness; and to godliness, brotherly kindness; and to brotherly kindness, love. For if you possess these qualities in increasing measure, they will keep you from being ineffective and unproductive in your knowledge of our Lord Jesus Christ. But if anyone does not have them, he is nearsighted and blind, and has forgotten that he has been cleansed from his past sins. (2 Peter 1:3–9)

Peter tells us that there will be people who know the Lord, but whose lives are "ineffective and unproductive." Their lives do not produce the harvest of good fruit that you would expect in the life of a believer. What has gone wrong? Well, Peter says that these people are missing the essential qualities of character (Christlikeness) that produce a good harvest (faith, goodness, knowledge, self-control, perseverance, godliness, brotherly kindness, and love). This leaves us with yet another question: Why would a believer not diligently pursue these things? Peter answers, "If anyone does not have them, he is nearsighted and blind, and has forgotten that he has been cleansed from his past sins."

Peter says that when you and I forget who we are, when we forget the magnitude of our sin and the glories of God's forgiveness, we will quit pursuing all that we have found in Christ. When you forget your sin and his forgiveness, you lose sight of the fact that apart from him, no good thing dwells in you. You begin to think of yourself as not being so bad, maybe even pretty good, on the whole. Your sins of talk start to look insignificant. You don't look at yourself, as Paul did near the end of his ministry, as the "worst" of sinners (1 Tim. 1:15). You lose your sense of gospel identity, and in so doing, any urgency for pursuing Christ.

At the beginning of this passage, Peter says two significant things about our identity as children of God. First, he wants us to know that our greatest problem is not evil without, but evil within. Christ came to save us, not just from the temptations of this fallen world, but from ourselves! He came so that we could "participate in the divine nature and escape the corruption in the world caused by evil desires." We needed rescue not only from the corruption of the world, but from the evil desires *of our own hearts* that make us susceptible to (and part of) this corruption. We needed to be saved from ourselves! The way that seemed right to us was death. We were enslaved to the cravings of the sinful nature. Our condition was so desperate, in fact, that Scripture says that no good thing could be found in us!

I am convinced that many believers lose sight of this. They see themselves as basically good and this perception radically affects their pursuit of Christ, as well as the way they respond to the sin of others. (See Luke 18:9–14, Christ's parable of the Pharisee and the tax collector.)

It also powerfully affects how they view their problems of the tongue. The tongue that James calls a "world of evil" simply doesn't seem that bad. However, people who understand the gospel not only rejoice in the deliverance from evil desires they have already experienced, but they sense their ongoing need for deliverance so that they can continue to live for him and not for themselves. They are not satisfied just with being saved; they long to stand before God, holy and blameless, to the praise of his glory. When this gospel identity grips your heart, you will not minimize your failures in communication. You will hunger to speak in a way that is honoring to Christ.

Peter's second point balances out the message. The gospel is not just about the magnitude of our sin, but about the overwhelming provisions of grace found in Christ. Peter says that we have been given "everything we need for life and godliness." Godliness means taking on the character of the Lord in my everyday life and relationships. Peter says, "Don't you know that the poverty of your sin has been overwhelmed by the glorious riches of his grace?" You have *everything* you need to live as God desires!

This is what produces a heart for Christ. I embrace the magnitude of my need, but also the lavishness of his provision. I want everything Christ has to offer me. I'm not satisfied with a little faith or a little goodness. I am not content with occasional moments of love. I do not want to keep struggling with self-control. I am not content with gossiping only a couple of times this month. I do not relax because I don't lash out in anger as much as I used to. I am not comfortable with the fact that I still tend to speak out of a selfish, bitter, or self-righteous heart. No, I hunger for more of what has been supplied to me in Christ!

This is the soil in which effective personal ministry grows. From here I can speak out of a sense of my own need and a deep appreciation for the work of Christ. I will not see myself as essentially different from you. I will recognize that God is not only working on you, but he is also working on me.

This is the way a repentant heart will be reflected in your talk. Your talk *can* be different! Your words *can* benefit others! Your communication *can* be God's tool of redemption and change. So turn to him in repentance. Take time to consider. Be humble in confession. Make concrete new commitments. Apply those commitments to your daily life and relationships and watch the Lord bless you with a harvest of good fruit.

Getting Personal:
Taking Time to Examine Your Heart

The psalmist prayed, "Search me, O God, and know my heart; test me and know my anxious thoughts. See if there is any offensive way in me, and lead me in the way everlasting" (Ps. 139:23–24). Take this moment as a God-given opportunity to discover any "offensive ways" in your communication. Ask God to show you the heart behind your words. Ask him to reveal where you have spoken out of fear, anger, doubt, vengeance, or selfishness. Ask God to show you how your words stand in the way of what he is doing. Ask what new attitudes need to fill your heart and direct your words. Seek God's forgiveness for blaming circumstances ("I wouldn't be upset if I didn't have so much to do today!"), others ("He drives me crazy!"), or even God ("If only I had known this earlier, I could have . . ."). Bask in the promises of forgiveness and deliverance that are found in the gospel!

Finally, commit yourself to a life of repentance. Be ready daily to go through the repentance cycle: (1) *Consider.* What things in your communication does God want you to see? (2) *Confess.* Where is God calling you to accept responsibility for your words and their consequences? What do you need to confess before God and others? (3) *Commit.* What new heart attitudes is God calling you to take on? What new ways of speaking is he calling you to? *(4) Change.* How do these new attitudes and actions need to be expressed in your daily life? Where must you now speak in a brand new way? Remember, God has *already* given you "everything you need for life and godliness" (2 Peter 1:3).

Chapter Twelve

Winning the War of Words

You must not give sin a vote in the way you conduct your lives. . . . Throw yourselves wholeheartedly and full-time—remember, you've been raised from the dead!—into God's way of doing things. (Rom. 6:11–13)

WE'VE identified the battle. It's not just a war of vocabulary or techniques. It is a war for the control of our hearts. Will we submit to the King, rest in his loving control, and seek to represent him in our relationships? For most of us this means repenting of a self-centeredness that causes our words to hinder the work of God. It means committing ourselves to a view that ministry is not one small aspect of our lives, but a lifestyle. This lifestyle reflects our calling by God to be his ambassadors in the everyday situations of life.

Our words are the principal tool God uses in the work he does through us. So we confess to our selfish, wandering hearts ("put off," Eph. 4:23–25) and we commit to ("put on") a new way of speaking, one that takes our calling seriously.

There is one more point to consider. How can you and I achieve a lasting victory in the war of words?

Words Matter; Words Can Destroy

I was in high school working my first job and dealing with a big problem outside the home for the first time. Co-workers were stealing and damaging property. I knew who was guilty, but the boss did not. I did not want to be part of what was going on, nor did I want to be blamed for something I did not do. I knew I needed to talk to my boss and possibly my co-workers, but I was afraid. I got up the courage to talk to my dad about what was happening. He agreed that I needed to talk to those involved, and then he said to me, "Be careful, son, to choose your words carefully." It was a nice way to summarize all that it means to communicate with purpose and control. My father was saying, "Paul, words matter. They will either contribute to a solution or further the difficulty. Speak with caution and care."

Winning the war of words involves choosing our words carefully. It is not just about the words we say, but also about the words we choose not to say. Winning the war is about being prepared to say the right thing at the right moment, exercising self-control. It is refusing to let our talk be driven by passion and personal desire but communicating instead with God's purposes in view. It is exercising the faith necessary to be part of what God is doing at that moment.

What Winning Looks Like

Galatians 5 explains in detail what it means to gain a lasting victory in the war of words.

> *You, my brothers, were called to be free. But do not use your freedom to indulge the sinful nature; rather, serve one another in love. The entire law is summed up in a single command: "Love your neighbor as yourself." If you keep on biting*

and devouring each other, watch out or you will be destroyed by each other.

So I say, live by the Spirit, and you will not gratify the desires of the sinful nature. For the sinful nature desires what is contrary to the Spirit, and the Spirit what is contrary to the sinful nature. They are in conflict with each other, so that you do not do what you want. But if you are led by the Spirit, you are not under law.

The acts of the sinful nature are obvious: sexual immorality, impurity and debauchery; idolatry and witchcraft; hatred, discord, jealousy, fits of rage, selfish ambition, dissensions, factions and envy; drunkenness, orgies, and the like. I warn you, as I did before, that those who live like this will not inherit the kingdom of God.

But the fruit of the Spirit is love, joy, peace, patience, kindness, goodness, faithfulness, gentleness and self-control. Against such things there is no law. Those who belong to Christ Jesus have crucified the sinful nature, with its passions and desires. Since we live by the Spirit, let us keep in step with the Spirit. Let us not become conceited, provoking and envying each other.

Brothers, if someone is caught in a sin, you who are spiritual should restore him gently. But watch yourself, or you also may be tempted. Carry each other's burdens, and in this way you will fulfill the law of Christ. (Gal. 5:13–6:2)

1. *Winning the war involves recognizing the destructive power of words (Gal. 5:15).* Paul warns us, "Watch out or you will be destroyed by each other." In the Garden of Eden we saw the life-altering power of words as the Serpent convinced Eve to eat the fruit. All over Scripture the importance of what we say and how we say it is depicted. We will never win the war of words as long as we minimize how critical a battle it is.

God has ordained us to be people of influence. Husband influences wife and vice versa. Parents influence children. Friend influences friend. Pastor influences his flock, and so on.

And the most powerful way we influence each other is through words, which encourage, rebuke, explain, teach, define, condemn, love, question, divide, unite, sell, counsel, judge, reconcile, war, worship, slander, and edify. People have influence and words have power. It is the way God meant it to be.

So we must never minimize our sins of communication. ("I didn't really mean it." "His bark is worse than his bite." "I just wasn't thinking." "She knows what I really think about her.") Paul reminds us that what we say has consequences. We are always representing the Lord. It is never okay to communicate in ways that contradict his message, methods, and character.

As I write this, it grieves me to think about the amount of talk in my family that does not recognize the seriousness Paul gives it here. No, we don't have "knock-down-drag-out" battles, but there is a lot of thoughtless, unkind, irritated, and complaining talk that slips by every day. I think we are like many Christian families—we minimize these "little" sins of talk because our home is free of physical and verbal abuse and we really do love one another. But Paul's words yank us back to reality. Words that "bite and devour" are words that destroy. They are not okay. So we must do all we can to assign words the importance Scripture gives them, remembering that God says we will give account of "every careless word" (Matt. 12:36).

2. *Winning the war means affirming our freedom in Christ (Gal. 5:13).* It is right to glory in the fact that God's grace frees us from the unbearable weight of the law (vv. 1–6). We are accepted into God's family solely on the basis of the righteous life, death, and resurrection of Jesus Christ. His righteousness has been assigned to our account. In this way we are happily free from the law.

But we cannot stop here. Affirming our freedom in Christ not only has a *from* aspect, but it has a *to* aspect as well. Paul says it this way: "But do not use your freedom to indulge the sinful nature." It is *never* biblical to say, "Because Jesus has freed me from the law, I can live any way I want." Any such idea completely misunderstands the purpose of grace. Paul wants us to affirm that our freedom makes it possible for us to live as we could not live before. We can actually live and speak in a way that pleases the Lord.

We have been freed not only from the requirement of the law for salvation, but from the bondage to sin in everyday living. We have been freed *from* the weight of the law *to* live a godly life. We cannot glory in what grace takes us *from* without also accepting what it calls us *to* (see Rom. 6:1–14; Titus 2:11–14).

Self-indulgent, sin-indulgent talk contradicts our identity as the children of grace. It turns us back toward the very bondage from which we have been freed. It forgets the position we have been given by Christ and the power he has given us by his Spirit. This leads to Paul's next point.

3. *Winning the war means saying no to the sinful nature (Gal. 5:13, 24).* This passage is very honest about what it is like to live in a fallen world as people who still sin. This includes members of Christian families!

When I was fifteen years old, my parents were away for a weekend, and my brother and I decided that our bedroom looked boring. It needed some decoration. We checked my father's workroom to see what kind of paint was available and found to our delight that he had many more colors than we would ever have imagined. We decided that the best way to apply the paint was to put it in small paper cups and throw it at the wall. For half an hour we "painted" the wall with mighty throws from several feet back. We thought it was a thing of beauty. We were so proud—that is, until our parents came home.

I will never forget the look on my dad's face as he saw our "beautiful" wall! It seemed like a torrent of emotion started at his feet and exploded from his mouth. His eyes flashed and his veins bulged. He screamed that we should throw the furniture out of the window and live like "hippies!" One of us mumbled that we didn't think the bed would fit. At that, he went ballistic! Out of his mouth came a tirade I will never forget.

What parent hasn't had to deal with a child doing something foolish and irresponsible? What wife hasn't been disappointed by her husband? What husband hasn't thought his wife has failed to give him his just due? What child has not felt misunderstood and mistreated by his parent? What sibling has not been hurt by a brother or sister? What friend has not been failed by a friend?

Which of us has not been provoked? Which of us has not been tempted to selfishness, to anger, to jealousy and greed? Which of us has not forsaken love to fight for some piece of the creation that we desperately wanted to possess? Galatians 5 is a sinners-in-a-world-of-sin passage. But it is more. This passage declares that we have power in Christ in the face of provocation.

In exhorting us not to indulge the sinful nature, Paul summarizes a powerful gospel reality that we do not want to miss. He says, "Those who belong to Christ have crucified the sinful nature with its *passions* and *desires*" (v. 24).

A passion is a fervent or intense emotion. A desire is something the heart craves. As sinners in a sinful world, we are going to experience both, Paul says. They will seem so powerful that we cannot act against them. This experience is exactly what Paul is addressing. What has Christ given us to help us deal with such intense temptations? Must we be controlled by what we feel and crave? These questions lead Paul to the work of Christ.

When Christ went to the cross, he did not purchase for us the *possibility* or *opportunity* to be saved. No, his work was personal, effective, and complete. It accomplished its purpose; it did not simply make salvation available as an option. Jesus went to the cross carrying the names of his children with him.

When Christ died, we died. When he was buried, we were buried with him. When he arose to newness of life, we rose with him. This is the truth we must grasp if we are ever to gain a lasting victory in the war of words. When Christ was crucified, my sinful nature (*with* its passions and desires) was crucified with him! I no longer live enslaved to sin. I no longer must submit to the intense emotions and the powerful cravings of my sinful nature.

The mastery of my sinful nature over me has been forever broken in Christ. For the first time, I can offer the parts of my body as instruments of righteousness—including my mouth (see Rom. 6:1–14). So Paul says, in effect (Gal. 5:13), "Don't indulge the sinful nature. Don't feed its passions and desires. Don't allow your words to be dictated by powerful feelings and cravings. Remember, because of what Christ has done, you have the power to say no."

Few truths are more important in winning the war for the heart. As sinners in a sinful world, we will be tempted and provoked, and in those moments powerful emotions and desires will grip us. But because of our identification with Christ, we have the power to say no. We *can* speak as his ambassadors even in the middle of real temptation and provocation! If we are living under the rule of emotion or the rule of desire, we are denying the gracious, rescuing work of our Savior.

There will be the little situations. Luella and I are in bed with sleep fast approaching and the phone rings. It is our son Justin at the train station. He needs a ride home. Luella says to me, "Won't you please go?" I am immediately hit with powerful emotions and powerful desires. I am frustrated that the call has come so late. I am irritated that it just happens to be the coldest night of the year. I feel as if it's always me who has to go. I want to stay in bed! I want someone else to be the chauffeur for a change.

If I allow my heart to be ruled by these emotions and desires, there is no way I will communicate as I should. My words will be selfish, angry, accusatory, and full of self-pity. But for this moment I have been given Christ. Sure, this is a little situation, but we all live in little moments like this. They really do determine the character of our talk.

Then there are the big situations. John was shocked when he came home one day to find his house emptied of everything but a bed, a lamp, and a kitchen table and chairs. His wife had been plotting to leave him for months. The moving van came while he was at work. On the table was a note with the number of her lawyer. In a few weeks she had secured permanent custody of the children.

It would be hard to describe the fear, rage, hurt, and sadness that gripped John as he stood in that empty house. In one moment his world had changed. He so much wanted to turn back the clock and give his wife what she really deserved. As he stood there, his emotions raged and his mind raced from thought to thought and desire to desire. In this moment, John's only hope was found in Christ. He *could* rise above his passions. He *could* say no to his desires. Even in *this* situation, he could speak as an ambassador of Christ. That hurt man went on to become a peacemaker. He spoke the truth in love. He overcame evil with good.

Many of us are quite skilled at living under the rule of sin's passions and desires. When we indulge them, our words add layers of interpersonal difficulty to the original problem. As we indulge the sinful nature we will tend to personalize what is not personal and turn moments of ministry into moments of irritation and anger. We will strike back at those we are meant to serve in order to satisfy ourselves. Self-indulgent talk never accomplishes God's purposes. It forgets the truths of the gospel and our identity as Christ's representatives. Paul reminds us that because of the work of Christ, we can do better.

Winning the war of words also means saying no to any rationalization, blame-shifting, or self-serving arguments that would excuse talk that flows out of the passions and desires of the sinful nature.

I remember the days when I was a young pastor of a struggling little congregation with huge counseling needs. It seemed I never had a quiet moment at home without someone calling me with the latest, greatest crisis. I dreaded hearing the phone ring at night and dreaded even more the words, "Paul, it's for you." Although I did not realize it, increasingly I saw certain people in the congregation as obstacles to what I wanted, rather than objects of the ministry I had gladly accepted from the Lord. I can remember getting calls, saying angrily to Luella, "Who is it *now*?" but then answering with a friendly, pastoral "Hello."

One Saturday afternoon I was relaxing at home with my wife and two young boys when I got a call from a desperate young man. He had been desperate for a long time and seemed to have the gift for calling me at all the wrong moments. He was always discouraged, always asking for help, yet always resistant to the help that was offered. Nothing seemed to work for him. He professed to have tried everything without benefit. He was at one of the seedy local motels, saying that he was going to end his life once and for all. He said that unless he had a reason to live, he would kill himself before the day was over. I found out where he was, asked my wife to pray, and got in my car to meet him.

I prayed on the way and I know that my wife was praying, but there was a war going on within. I *was* that catalog of conflicting desires! I really disliked this man. I disliked his humped-shouldered posture. I disliked his whiny voice. I disliked his need to always be the center of someone's attention. I hated the way he spit back at me every insight I had ever offered. I resented the time he had taken away from my family and other aspects of my ministry. And I was angry that I had to go once more and put him back together. As I drove, my thoughts were pulled back and forth in the war between pastoral concern and personal resentment.

I arrived at the motel and we sat in a dingy room that smelled of smoke and sweat. He gave me his normal litany of complaints. I began to respond with truths from the gospel when he interrupted me and said, "You're not going to trot out that stuff again, are you? Don't you have anything new to say?" I couldn't believe what I was hearing. Here I had left my family out of concern for him, and he mocked my efforts to help without any evidence of appreciation! I lost it, giving in to the rage that had been building for weeks. I verbally tore him limb from limb. I told him exactly what the congregation and I thought of him. I laid as much guilt on him as I could, told him to get off his duff and do something right for a change, prayed for him (!), and left! I was seething as I drove away.

It didn't take long for conviction to set in. It also didn't take long for rationalization and self-excusing arguments to set in right behind. By the time I arrived home, I was convinced that I had spoken like one of the prophets of old, proclaiming a "thus says the Lord" in a sinful and rebellious place. I had convinced myself that God would use this dramatic moment of truth-speaking to create lasting change in this man's life.

I arrived home and Luella (who had been praying) asked me how the time had gone. I told her that I had spoken to him more strongly than I had ever spoken to anyone in my ministry, being careful to use the prophet analogy with her. She immediately said, "It sounds to me like you got angry and blew it." The moment she said these words, I saw my self-serving rationalizations for what they were. I was filled with remorse. As it turned out, my subsequent confession to this man of my own sin and struggle was what God used to begin to turn him around.

4. *Winning the war means speaking to serve others in love (Gal. 5:13–14).* We say no to the rule of passions and desires not only because Christ gives us the power to do so, but also because we have been called to serve. The opposite of indulging the sinful nature is not saying, "I must not, I must not, I must not." We are called to *put off* self-indulgent talk to *put on* talk that flows out of a love for others.

Paul could not make the call here any stronger. He tells us that the "entire law" is summarized by this one command: Love your neighbor as yourself. Speaking in a way that serves the needs of others is at the heart of God's will for us, and his enabling grace makes it possible.

The picture in this passage is of a God who is relentlessly at work by his Spirit, conforming his people to the image of his Son. He wants to use us to accomplish that purpose. This is part of my calling each time I speak.

Serving in love does not mean that I become a slave to the agenda of everyone around me. It does not mean being a doormat. Rather, it means living with redemptive purpose. Love desires another's highest good. The highest good I could desire for anyone is that he or she would become like Christ, that is, take on the fruit of the Spirit. God does this work in the normal events and relationships of daily life. He works for this good in every situation (see Rom. 8:28–30).

Ephesians 4:29 describes what it means to speak out of love: "Do not let any unwholesome talk come out of your mouths, but only what is helpful for building others up according to their needs, that it may benefit those who listen." Unwholesome talk forgets the other person and concentrates on what I feel and what I want. But Paul calls us to talk that is other-oriented.

If I am going to serve another with my words, Paul says there are three things to consider: (1) I must consider the *person* ("only what is helpful for building others up"). What do I know about this individual that would shape what I say? (2) I must consider the *problem* ("according to their needs"). What is this person's real need in this situation, and how should it guide what I say? (3) I must consider the *process* ("that it may benefit those who listen"). I am not just spouting off. My communication should have a redemptive purpose; it should benefit the listener.

Frankly, in our own strength, none of us are this nice! Sin makes us intensely selfish people. We instinctively think about our own needs and wants. We are primarily committed to our own welfare. But as we humbly admit our selfishness, we can begin to appreciate and rely upon the enabling grace of Christ. He *has* broken the mastery of our sinful passions and desires. He *does* equip us by his Spirit to speak as his ambassadors. We *can* speak out of a commitment to serve others in love.

Winning the war of words comes from serving. Winning comes from loving, from talk that is free from bondage to me (my passions and desires) and is therefore free to minister to you.

5. *Winning the war means speaking "in step with the Spirit" (Gal. 5:25).* Keeping in step with the Spirit means speaking in a way that reflects his work in me and encourages his work in you. In this passage the Spirit's work is made quite clear. He is working to produce in us a harvest consistent with the character of Christ: love, joy, peace, patience, kindness, goodness, faithfulness, gentleness, and self-control. As an act of faith and submission, I hold my speaking up to the standard of this fruit. I look at difficult situations as God-given opportunities to see this fruit mature in me. Problems are not obstacles to the development of this fruit, but opportunities to see it grow.

Years ago, there was a man in our congregation who was particularly critical of my ministry (not that it was without need of criticism!). I struggled inside whenever I saw this man or even thought of him. I remember being relieved when I would arrive at a church event to find that he was not there. I was also aware that he was not keeping his opinion of me to himself, but had begun to gather together a group of malcontents who shared his views. Our congregation was not large and the discontent was becoming more and more obvious.

I decided that it was time to ask this man if we could talk. I told my wife about my plan, and she immediately asked me what I intended to say. As I shared my thoughts with her, I could sense that she was responding negatively, and so I asked her what was wrong. She said, "Before you can deal with him, Paul, you have to deal with yourself. It sounds like you hate this man. I don't think any good can come out of confronting him with his wrong until you deal with your own attitudes."

I wanted to think that Luella was just another person who was misunderstanding and misjudging me, but she wasn't. I did hate this man. I hated the controlling effect he had on me. I hated the fact that he had turned others against me. I hated the way his criticism caused me to second-guess everything I did as a pastor! I hated how he had destroyed my dream for my ministry and our congregation. I hated the arrogant smirk on his face. I didn't really want to deal with him—I just wanted him out of my life!

Luella was right. I was in no condition to be an instrument of the Spirit in his life. I was in no position to win the war of words. I *was* totally out of step with the Spirit in regards to this relationship. I *did* need to deal with me first. I *did* need to examine my heart, confess the sin that was there, and determine to speak in a way that reflected the fruit the Spirit was working in me.

As I examined my heart, I saw that there was more that needed to change than I had ever thought. My problem was not just hatred and anger, but heart sins at an even deeper level. What had been motivating me in ministry was not the work of the Lord, but my personal dream. I had dreamed of going into a tough area to minister and being successful in a way no one else had been. I had dreamed of being highly respected by a growing congregation and, before long, the entire Christian community. I had dreamed of great numerical growth, of building a large, modern facility, and of leading the "mover-and-shaker" church in the region. Most of all, I had dreamed of being known as the one at the center of it all.

I hated this man because he was *right*! He was not right in the way he had dealt with his concerns about my ministry, but he was right in his insight into my pride. I *did* enjoy being at the center of every gathering. I *did* have the final opinion on every topic. I *was* frustrated when people would get in the way of my novel programs. I hated how slowly things moved and how negative people were. And I struggled with God for putting me in this hard place.

The very man I hated I now began to see as an instrument of rescue in God's hands. It was through "Pete" (not his real name) that my selfish, arrogant dream was exposed and began to die. Under the heat of this trial God showed me the sin in my heart in a new way. As I took several days to examine this situation and my own heart, I began to be thankful for the very man I had hated. I wasn't thankful for his sin, but thankful for how God had used him in my life. As I became thankful, I began to listen to what Pete had said about me and how he had said it. As I considered the content of his words, I realized that there were things that God wanted me to learn—yes, even from this harsh messenger. And as I listened to the way he communicated his thoughts, I discovered that he and I were a lot alike. Pete was proud, opinionated, vocal, and impatient. I had hated all of those things, but they were present in me as well.

During those days God gave me a genuine, pastoral love for Pete. When we finally talked, I was able to communicate to him in a way that was patient, kind, gentle, peaceful, and self-controlled. I was even able to go into this difficult talk with joy as I thought about the good that the Spirit had done in me through him.

Speaking in step with the Spirit not only means speaking in a way that reflects what the Spirit is doing in me, but it also means encouraging the Spirit's fruit in you. Frankly, I didn't care at first if God used me in Pete's life or not. There were only two things I cared about: I wanted to prove Pete wrong, and I wanted him to leave our church and me alone! I had fallen into thinking that my struggle *was* with "flesh and blood" (see Eph. 6:10–12). I saw Pete as the enemy and lost sight of the spiritual warfare going on beneath the difficulties of this relationship. I did not want to serve Pete; I wanted him to be a supporter of my dream. Even as his pastor, the last thing I had in mind was being a tool of redemption in his life. In fact, I never even considered how I could be the Spirit's instrument in his life until my talk with Luella.

When I finally met with Pete, I had a radically different agenda from the one I had first discussed with my wife. I no longer wanted to "win." I no longer wanted him to shut up and get on board with my dream. I really did want to be used of God to encourage the fruit of the Spirit in his life.

Pete came to our talk ready for battle. It was clear that he had prepared his weapons and rehearsed his defenses. But there was no battle. I told him that I was thankful for his insights; that through him the Spirit had really exposed my heart, and I asked for his forgiveness. Before I ever had a chance to talk about him, he said, "Paul, I've been wrong too. I guess if I were honest I would have to say that I have hated you, and I have looked for every opportunity to criticize you to others. I have been angry with you and angry with God for putting us in this congregation. I need your forgiveness."

That night, for the first time in a long while, Pete and I spoke in step with the Spirit, and the Spirit produced new growth in each of us. But don't miss the point: it started with someone confronting me and encouraging me to examine my *own* heart before I confronted someone else. Speaking in step with the Spirit means taking time to listen, examine, reflect, and prepare. It means communicating in a way that promotes the Spirit's work of grace in our lives and others.

6. *Winning the war means speaking with a goal to restore (Gal. 6:1–2).* Paul says, "Brothers, if someone is caught in a sin, you who are spiritual should restore him gently. . . ." Let's be sure we understand these words. Notice first that Paul does not say, "*If you catch* someone in a sin. . . ." He is not talking about sneaking up on someone to catch him in the act! Rather, he is talking about how we as sinners get "caught"—that is, entrapped and ensnared in sin.

Sin is deceitful. The Devil is a schemer who will whisper "fine-sounding arguments" in our ears (Col. 2:4) to convince us that what we are doing is okay. Sin is a snare that tightens its hold on us *as* we believe those "fine-sounding arguments" and use them to rationalize and justify what we've done. Before we know it, we are in deeper bondage to the sin than we ever dreamed possible. And we don't even know how we got there!

All of us are prone to sin this side of glory. We get "caught" in anger, pride, self-pity, envy, vengeance, self-righteousness, bitterness, lust, selfishness, fear, disbelief, etc. And we either don't even know that we are caught or we don't know how to extricate ourselves. In one way or another we all live "caught" in some aspect of our lives all the time. There are areas of sin we are blind to, sins that are our particular theme of struggle. There *will* be a day when the final snare falls off and we will be with Christ and like him forever! But until that time we need to recognize that as sinners we are "catchable," and for that reason, we need one another.

Paul then says, "You who are spiritual should restore him gently." Is he talking about some super-spiritual elite corps of restorers? No, not at all! This word "spiritual" is not being used to refer only to a biblically mature person. It really embraces *every believer.* It is referring back to Galatians 5:25, where Paul said that we are to "keep in step with the Spirit," that is, to be sensitive to what the Spirit is doing in us and others. When we are "keeping in step with the Spirit" we position ourselves to serve as his restorers. All of us, if we are living lives worthy of our calling, are positioning ourselves to be God's agents of rescue and restoration.

Winning the war of words means letting this restoration agenda shape and direct our relationships. The temptation for all of us is to mistakenly believe that our relationships belong to us. We tend to view other people as our possessions. Parents fall into this with their children. Then, in the teenage years, when the child fails, the parents can't see beyond their own anger and hurt to be agents of restoration for their own offspring!

We tend to see others as existing for our own happiness. Husbands and wives come to believe that it is their mate's responsibility to make them happy. They watch their spouse with vigilant, expectant eyes. Life becomes a series of final exams, and yet the happiness they seek never comes. We all tend to look at the people around us with an eye to how they are responding to us, how they are affecting us. We look for proper respect, love, appreciation, acceptance, and honor, and we find it very hard to continue in relationships where it does not exist.

Paul is calling us to something radically different here. He is calling us to the new and higher agenda for our relationships that this book describes. This new agenda is rooted in the fundamental recognition that our relationships (and the people in them) do not belong to us but to God. He owns us as Creator and has reclaimed us as Savior. Christ has purchased the condemned house (us!). He has moved in and is now at work doing a complete restoration. This is the gospel foundation for relationships in the body of Christ. It is vital that we understand our position. We do not, nor will we ever, own these relationships for ourselves. We are tools in the hands of the true Owner, who is busy in the work of restoration.

Once we learn to see our relationships this way, we will begin to see the need for restoration all around us. When you're taking a vacation and the children are quarreling in the back seat, there is more going on than your expensive vacation being ruined! The need for restoration is revealing itself. You can respond to this situation as an irritated parent or as a restorer who wants to be used by the great Restorer. When you are having coffee with a friend and he is complaining once again about his boss, wondering why God hasn't done something, there is more going on than a nice evening being ruined. Here again, God is calling you to more than self-pity. He has positioned you to be a restorer.

When husbands and wives disagree over the same old stuff once again, they need to do more than curse the fact that their marriage just doesn't work or that the other person never seems to have a clue. The need for restoration is made clear by these themes of struggle. They need to see where they are "caught," and they need to respond to one another, not with a demand agenda, but with a restoration agenda.

When your relationship with your teenager has gotten cold, distant, and hostile, it is not time to wallow in self-pity, rehearsing all the things that you have done for him over the years with little respect and thanks. It is not time to give in to verbal wars or to build the icy walls of bitterness. It is time to see the need for restoration. Your teenager is "caught" (maybe you are too!), and he is in desperate need of restoration. But you will not be a tool of restoration as long as you demand that he meet your expectations of relational happiness.

When your supper table disintegrates into a war zone of competition and petty conflicts, it is not time to lash out in anger or pick up your plate to eat in another room. Your children are demonstrating that they are "caught," and God has positioned you to be used in restoration work that evening.

Winning the war of words means speaking redemptively, and speaking redemptively is rooted in a restoration perspective on relationships. The purpose of human relationships is not human happiness. It is the work of reconciling people to God and restoring them to the image of his Son.

Winning the war of words means never forgetting who we are. When we remember that we are what we are because of God's mercy alone, we speak with gentleness and humility as God's restorers. How often our talk to one another lacks this gentleness and humility! We fail to speak redemptively because we have forgotten who *he* is and what he is doing in our relationships. We fail to speak with gentleness and humility because we have forgotten who *we* are and our own dependency on his grace.

Winning Is a Journey

Galatians 5 pictures people on a journey who are focused not just on what they have to carry, but on who else needs assistance. This is how the passage ends (6:2). With the words, "Carry each other's burdens," Paul broadens his call to us. Winning the war of words is not only about rescuing the one who is ensnared in sin, but about being attentive to all the places where you may struggle. In the journey of life, I am not just focused on balancing my own load properly, but my eyes are on you, too. When I see a person struggling to carry his load, I am called to share the weight. This is the love Christ talked about in John 13:34, the "royal law" of James 2:8. The way of Christ is never selfish, never self-absorbed. Christ's love is other-directed, other-focused, and self-sacrificing.

So we are called to support one another as we journey through this fallen world. We are called to speak to one another out of this "burden-bearing" mentality. When we see people struggling with weakness, we point them to the strength available in Christ. When someone is ignorant, we speak with wisdom-giving words of truth. When someone is fearful, we talk of God, who is an ever-present help in trouble. When people grieve, we seek to comfort. When they are discouraged, we seek to bring words of hope. When they feel alone, we remind them of our love and Christ's presence. When they are angry, we point them to a God of righteousness, vengeance, and justice. In the midst of conflict, we seek to speak as peacemakers and reconcilers. When people are anxious, we point them to the Sabbath rest Christ has given his children.

Winning the war of words means living with eyes open, aware not only of our own struggle, but of other pilgrims struggling on the journey with us. In so doing, we all come to realize that we are not alone. Christ has planned for the many hands of his people to join together to make an otherwise impossible load bearable. We need not despair, quit, or run in the other direction. Rather, strengthened and encouraged, we continue the journey.

Winning the war means choosing our words carefully. We do not want to give any room in our talk to the passions and desires of the sinful nature. In our own conceit and envy, we do not want to provoke one another to sin. We do not want to bite and devour one another with words. Rather, we are committed to serve one another in love with all of our talk. We want to speak in step with what the Spirit is producing in us and in others. We want to speak in a way that encourages the growth of that fruit. Finally, we want to speak as gentle, humble agents of restoration, as burden-bearers committed to live by Christ's rule of love.

What radical revival, reconciliation, and restoration would result if we carried this call into every relationship in our lives! How different things would be if we were consistently committed to this kind of communication! How transformed our relationships would be if we spoke to one another with words of redemption! A commitment to winning the war of words calls us to choose our words well.

Getting Personal: Strategies for War

1. Where in your communication do you tend to forget your freedom in Christ and wind up indulging the sinful nature? (With your spouse, boss, parents, siblings, neighbor, extended family, body of Christ?) Take time to identify your personal battlefields.

2. List the powerful emotions and desires to which you need to say no. (Examples of emotions: anger, discouragement, fear. Examples of desires: vengeance, respect, appreciation, control, success, love.)

3. In what specific areas is God calling you to speak out of a commitment to serve others in love?

4. Which fruit of the Spirit needs to grow in you and more consistently influence the way you talk to others? (patience, self-control, kindness, joy)

5. Where do you see restorative work that needs to be done around you? How can your words help? What daily opportunities do you have to be part of what God is doing in others?

Remember, because of what Christ has done, we *can* say no to the passions and desires of the sinful nature. We *can* serve each other in love even in the face of provocation.

Chapter Thirteen

Choosing Your Words

Post this at all the intersections, dear friends: Lead with your ears, follow up with your tongue, and let anger straggle along in the rear. (James 1:19)

I sat in my family room and I was steaming! I couldn't believe that after all the years of love, all our efforts to understand, and all the investments we had made in building a relationship of mutual trust, he was willing to throw it all away for one night of fun with his friends. I couldn't imagine how this night could be that important to him.

My son had looked me in the face and lied to me. I was so angry! I wanted him to hurt the way I did. I wanted to give him what he deserved. In my mind I rehearsed a toe-to-toe confrontation with him. (All in the name of the Lord, of course!) I contemplated a series of grave punishments that would alter his life indefinitely. I just wished he were home so I could get it over with. I told Luella, "He'll regret the day he ever thought of doing this to me!"

I sat there steaming, but not just because my son had lied and was not home for me to punish. I was also upset because Luella completely disagreed with the way I wanted to handle him. *She's just too soft,* I reasoned to myself. *It's for times like these that God called me to be the spiritual leader of this family. Somebody needs to stand for the truth! Someone needs to confront the wrong that's taken place here.*

However, the more I sat there defending my anger and rehearsing what I would do to my son, the weaker my resolve became. You see, God in his awesome wisdom had ordained that my son would be out of the house at this time. God was the one who sent my wife as an agent of intervention. God had to deal with me before he could use me in my son's life.

It wasn't long before I was no longer thinking about my son, but about myself. I was grieved at what I saw. After all the years of Bible study and ministry, all the years of counseling and teaching, and all the years of personal Bible study and prayer, how could I be here once again, eaten up by my own anger? Hurt and ready to hurt back?

That afternoon, alone in the family room, I was once again confronted with something we tend to forget or seriously minimize—the presence and power of indwelling sin. I became aware once again that the process of sanctification was not over for me. The great spiritual battle for my heart rages on. But I was also aware that God was powerfully at work, controlling the scene and raising up my wife to give me time to examine my thoughts, motives, and behavior. I saw that I needed the Lord that day just as much as the first day I believed.

Maybe I was experiencing the only really honest mix of emotions in the Christian life. Grief mixed with joy, mourning tempered by rejoicing, and helplessness mixed with glorious hope. They all picture the truth that where sin abounds, grace abounds all the more. Awareness of the magnitude of my personal sin must be overwhelmed by my acknowledgment of God's active, forgiving, and delivering grace. Any real appreciation of the glories of grace will come only as I grasp the depth and power of indwelling sin.

The war rages on! This is why we must choose our words carefully. We *are* prone to wandering away. We *are* controlled by our raging passions. We *are* still easily taken captive by sinful desires. We *do* get tricked again and again by evil's deceitful scheming, which tempts us to lose our gospel moorings.

Preparing to Choose the Right Words

By the time my son came home the next night, I was in a different place. I had done four things that prepared me to deal with the situation. Here's what I did:

1. *I confessed my need to God.* It was important for me to see that these situations not only reveal the other person's spiritual need, but my own need as well. If we are ever going to choose words that allow us to be God's instruments of change, we have to start by acknowledging our own need of his grace. In our own strength we will not be what he meant us to be, or do what he called us to do. Only by his grace do we have any hope of wholesome talk in times of provocation. We need to begin by confessing to God the attitudes that stand in the way of what he wants to do through us.

2. *I acknowledged God's grace to me.* We must not give in to thoughts that real change is impossible. This is a denial of the gospel we say we believe. Proper acknowledgment of the resources of God's grace will always result in the courage of faith. This in turn will result in decisive actions of faith. When we lose sight of our identity as the recipients of God's grace, we become ineffective and unproductive (2 Peter 1:8–9), running from, rather than slaying, the Goliaths in our lives. But acknowledging grace means that I live as if I really do believe that he already has given me, in Christ, everything I need—not just for eternal life, but for godly living in this fallen world (2 Peter 1:3–4). I needed to acknowledge his grace that evening.

3. *I said, "No!"* If we have acknowledged our need and the provision of Christ's grace, then we know we can say no to the desires and passions of the sinful nature (Gal. 5:13–15,

24–25). We no longer live under sin's control. It is no longer our master (Rom. 6:1–14), so we can "put to death" its desires and deeds (Rom. 8:1–17). We need to identify the specific passions and desires that move us away from what God is calling us to do and say. We need to commit ourselves once more to him, so that we will not allow these things to be our functional masters. My wife was right. Before I talked to our son, I needed to say no to ungodly attitudes and desires.

4. *I said, "Thank you!"* In saying "thank you" to God, we are acknowledging our calling and recognizing the opportunity he has given us to be part of what he is doing in the lives of others. A thankful spirit reminds us that these are not our moments but his; he has chosen us out of the mass of humanity to be his ambassadors. This is a great privilege. Our lives have eternal meaning and purpose. We have a reason to get up in the morning! We have the opportunity to be a strategic part of his grand plan of redemption. What an identity! The only proper response is worship.

As we prepare to speak to one another, the storm of human emotion needs to be calmed by the rest and hope of worship. He is here! He is already at work! His grace is sufficient! Sin is no longer in control! He has called me and strategically placed me here, and in his strength I can do what he is calling me to do. Yes, the seas are violently raging, but the Messiah is in the boat with me! There is hope for me and for you! This rest and this hope will allow us to choose our words wisely.

Choosing Your Words

Perhaps you are thinking, *Paul, I'm not sure what you mean when you say we need to choose our words. Should we rehearse ahead of time all the specific things we will say? That seems a little unrealistic.* I would agree. Choosing your words does not mean writing a script for every conversation. Rather, it means being *redemp-*

tively intentional. If my purpose (intention) is to function as God's representative, then I need to take time to consider what that means practically in this circumstance with this person. Much of the damage we do with our talk occurs because we have not prepared in this way.

Ephesians 4 is a simple, practical guide for what it means to choose our words wisely. It can guide our discussion of the words that will encourage God's work in others. What *are* the words we must choose?

Choosing Words of Truth

As Paul reminds the Ephesian Christians of their call to daily ministry, he calls them to "speak the truth in love." I am persuaded that we often miss the point of what Paul is saying here. Typically we see it as a call for two people to be lovingly honest with each other. Certainly this is very important, but it is not what this passage is teaching. Let's look at the content of this command.

> *Then we will no longer be infants, tossed back and forth by the waves, and blown here and there by every wind of teaching and by the cunning and craftiness of men in their deceitful scheming. Instead, speaking the truth in love, we will in all things grow up into him who is the Head, that is, Christ. (Eph. 4:14–15)*

Notice that Paul is not focusing on the danger of *dishonesty*, but the danger of *falsehood*. He wants the church in Ephesus to have the functional stability that only the truth of God can give. Paul recognizes that the enemy is a schemer who works to unsettle God's people with the conflicting, ever-changing winds of falsehood. His call here is not for a formal theology class, but for the doctrines of Scripture to shape the way we think about everyday events. His concern is that we would be mature enough to choose words of truth, and that we would be more zealous to communicate biblical truth than our own perspectives and opinions.

God has given us his truth so that it would make sense out of life for us. He knew that we would never properly understand life on our own. He also knew that in this fallen world, there would be a din of voices, all vying for our hearts, all considering the same set of facts, yet each giving them a very different meaning. God's Word was given to cut through all the confusion and exegete life for us. It is vital that we speak biblical truth to one another daily. As we do, we will mature in Christ.

If this is our commitment, there are several questions we need to ask ourselves regularly.

1. *What truths of Scripture (doctrines, themes, commands, principles, perspectives, metaphors, etc.) interpret and explain this situation?* This first question is important, because we have seen that we do not respond to life based on the facts of a given situation, but on our interpretation of those facts. Therefore, we must be careful to interpret things biblically and help others to do the same. In my counseling, I do this more than anything else. I am often distressed by how difficult it is for people to do this on their own. Sadly, the results are evident in their lives.

2. *What does God want to show this person about himself, his love and grace, his will, and his truth?* If God is in each situation as an ever-present, helping Redeemer, then the situation reveals things about him. The problem in any situation is not that God is absent or inactive but that we tend to be blind to his presence and work. We are often like the servant of Elisha who was terrified as the enemy surrounded them. I love the way Elisha spoke to his fear. He said, "Those who are with us are more than those who are with them." Then he prayed, "O LORD, open his eyes so he may see." When the servant looked

again, he saw the hills full of celestial horses and chariots of fire (2 Kings 6:8–23)!

Often people say to me, "I don't understand why God isn't working in my life. Why doesn't he answer my prayers? Why doesn't he help me?" These questions reflect blindness to the Lord's presence and work. We need to help others see the Lord and their situation with biblical eyes. And we need to do this in humility, with an awareness of our own spiritual blindness and similar need.

3. *What does God want to show this person about himself?* Situations of life not only reveal the Lord, but they reveal much about us as well. God uses these moments so that we would not be tricked by the deceitfulness of sin, but would see ourselves with biblical clarity. The truth of biblical self-evaluation is a painful gift we all need. It is the kind of "wound" that a faithful friend will give (Prov. 27:6). To help people see themselves clearly, we need to hold up the mirror of the Word of God before them. What *we* think of them is unimportant, what Scripture reveals about them is true and essential. We want to be used by God to knock down a few more bricks off their wall of self-deception, recognizing that this is a process and not a one-time event. We can be thankful for the opportunity to make a little more progress.

4. *What does God want to show this person about others?* Our view of others is also distorted by sin. We need to help people bring biblical clarity to the way they think about other people.

5. *What is God calling this person to do?* We want to lead people to joyfully do his will in their specific situations. What is God's agenda for this person? What is he calling him or her to think, desire, and do?

6. *How can I best help this person to understand these things?* When we think practically, we think methodologically. Finger-

pointing lectures are counterproductive. So is the recitation of biblical platitudes unexplained and unapplied. Most "if I were you" talk is counterproductive. What we want to do first is to incarnate the wonderful love of the Lord we represent (see Col. 3:12–14). We want people to see *him,* to rest in him and follow him.

Next, we want to build a bridge of understanding between the truths of Scripture and the realities of the particular situation. How can we best build that bridge? What questions can we ask? What passages would be helpful? What stories can we tell? What examples (metaphors) would give understanding? What do we know about this person that would help us make wise choices here? (Jesus was a master at this.)

We want to choose words of truth, but this means more than being honest. It means being distinctively biblical in the way we respond to others.

Choosing Words of Love

Paul qualifies his call to speak words of truth (biblical perspective) by reminding us that this truth must be spoken in love. No qualifier could be more important. Truth that is not spoken in love ceases to be truth because it becomes distorted by human impatience, bitterness, and anger.

Being committed to speaking the truth in love means being committed to keeping truth untainted by the passions and desires of the sinful nature. It means being committed to be part of what the Spirit is seeking to do in another person's life. I am more committed to his work than to my own desires. I am willing to die to self so that in my speaking I may live for him.

There are no more practical directions for choosing words of love than Paul's definition of love in 1 Corinthians 13.

> *Love is patient, love is kind. It does not envy, it does not boast, it is not proud. It is not rude, it is not self-seeking, it is*

not easily angered, it keeps no record of wrongs. Love does not delight in evil but rejoices with the truth. It always protects, always trusts, always hopes, always perseveres. (vv. 4–7)

The call to this standard is found all over the New Testament. Before his death, Jesus' final words to his disciples were a "new command" to love one another as he had loved them (John 13:34–35). This love would identify them as his disciples. It can be found in Romans 12:9–21, in the call to sincere love in the face of evil. We see it in Ephesians 4:2 as Paul calls us to "be completely humble and gentle; be patient, bearing with one another in love." This standard is held up for us in Philippians 2:1–4, where we are told to "do nothing out of selfish ambition or vain conceit, but in humility consider others better than yourselves," and in Colossians 3, where Paul says, "Clothe yourselves with compassion, kindness, humility, gentleness and patience. Bear with each other and forgive whatever grievances you may have against one another . . ." (vv. 12–13).

Listen to the talk that goes on in your home. How much of it is impatient and unkind? How often are words spoken out of selfishness and personal desire? How easily do outbursts of anger occur? How often do we bring up past wrongs? How do we fail to communicate hope? How do we fail to protect? How often do our words carry threats that we have "had it" and are about to quit? Stop and listen, and you will see how much we need to hold our talk to this standard of love, and how often the truth we profess to speak has been distorted by our sin.

It is time for many of us to confess that we have not known the way of love. Our words have hindered, not helped, what the Lord is seeking to do. We have been controlled by the passions and desires of the sinful nature and failed to represent Christ's character. We need to cry out for grace to speak loving words as his ambassadors.

As I prepared to talk to my son, I prayed that my words would meet the biblical standard of love. I confessed my anger, impatience, and pride. As I did so, my feelings radically changed. I entered his room with hope, and the feeling that a great burden had been lifted. I was still upset and concerned about what he had done, but I was able to speak quietly and without anger. That night truth was heard more loudly than my anger. For that I was very thankful—and so was my son!

Choosing Words of Restraint

One of the most significant yet neglected biblical character qualities is self-control. So much of our trouble with talk has to do with our failure in this area. Words are spoken that should never have been uttered. They are spoken at the wrong time, in the wrong place, or with emotions that are raging out of control. Words are spoken when silence would have been a more godly, loving choice. They are more driven by personal desire and demand than the purposes of God or the needs of others. The problem? A lack of self-control, the internal restraint system that reflects the indwelling presence of the Holy Spirit. Paul says it this way: "You, however, are not controlled by the sinful nature but by the Spirit, if the Spirit of God lives in you" (Rom. 8:9). Self-control is a fruit of his work. We no longer need to be led around by the cravings of the sinful nature. This surely includes our talk!

As a practical act of faith in the Spirit's work within us, we need to be committed not only to words of truth and love, but also to words of restraint. Such words flow from the self-control that the Spirit has given us. Paul has important things to say in Ephesians 4 about words of restraint.

> *Therefore each of you must put off falsehood and speak truthfully to his neighbor, for we are all members of one body. "In your anger do not sin": Do not let the sun go down while you are still angry, and do not give the devil a foothold. (vv. 25–27)*

Paul is saying, "When you speak, exercise the self-control that belongs to you as a child of God. Don't give in to the pull of the sinful nature's passions and desires. You have been made new in Christ. Here is a place to live out that newness. Speak words of restraint in the face of provocation." According to Paul, what does this restraint look like?

1. *Words of restraint are honest.* Paul says it plainly, "Put off falsehood and speak truthfully." This is the only way of love. Whenever I am dishonest or "trim" or shade the truth, I am loving myself more than God or others. Trimming the truth is saying less than needs to be said. Dishonesty occurs when we look out for ourselves first. I want your respect or acceptance, so I trim the truth to hide my faults. I want your trust and confidence, so I am dishonest about my failings. I find confrontation distasteful, so I avoid issues that lead to conflict. There are things I want from you, so I shade the details to my advantage. I do not want the embarrassment of confessing wrong to you, so I cast past events in a light that is favorable to me. I do not want you to know that I failed you, so I concoct some acceptable excuse. Truth is the casualty when I love myself more than I love you.

We need to recognize how powerful our desires are for self-protection, for ease and comfort, for vindication, for acceptance and approval, for love. How much we want to be the center of attention, to live free of conflict, and to have our desires and dreams fulfilled!

But speaking the truth means exercising self-control over this powerful draw to self-love. It means that I will not sacrifice personal truth for personal ease. I will not buy what I want with the currency of falsehood. Instead, I will exercise the gift of self-control over the desires of my sinful nature, placing myself in God's capable hands, speaking honest words, no matter what the consequences may be. Words of restraint are self-controlled in honesty.

I should add here that such relational honesty must also meet the demands of love previously considered. Often, "honest" words are far from restrained words of love. Instead, they are vengeful weapons in an ever-escalating, destructive war of words. They never build up because they are meant to tear down. They are hurled at someone viewed as the enemy. Their goal is never to help but to win the relational war. This kind of "honesty" could not be further from what Paul calls us to here.

2. *Words of restraint are not controlled by anger.* There is no place where Paul's confidence in Christ's indwelling power is more obvious than here. He actually believes that we can exercise restraint in moments of anger! In the place where the Devil is often given a huge foothold, Paul believes that his wicked work can be thwarted, and the Lord's work can be done. Paul assumes that it is possible to be angry without sin. Not all anger is sinful, but Paul's counsel is this: "In these moments of powerful emotion, when you feel as if you have lost all control, exercise the internal restraint you have been given as a child of God."

How tempting it is to give in to thoughts of helplessness, forgetting the indwelling presence of the Spirit! Consider the Christian mother who is in a screaming match with her teenage son when the phone rings. She turns from what appeared to be an out-of-control verbal barrage and answers the phone with a lilting, "Hel-lo-o." She has chosen, for selfish reasons, to exercise the self-control *that had been possible all along.* She had also chosen, before the phone rang, to give in to the passions and desires of the sinful nature in her argument with her son. We are confronted here with the power Christ has given us to speak as he has called us to speak. Cling to him! The restraint we need is found in him; it is not a technique acquired in a communication course.

Paul alludes to two typical but opposite anger reactions that call for self-control. First, some of us are tempted to *blow up* when we are angry, venting raging emotions and letting words fly without any control. This is my tendency. I have never hurt anyone by my silence! Rather, I am a verbal person and most of my sin struggles in relationships have been struggles with words.

But I am learning the importance of walking away, of waiting, and of preparation. I have learned, through the example of my wife, that I am able to exercise internal restraint even when I am quite upset.

One afternoon the two of us were having a conversation in our kitchen that began to anger me. Luella suggested that we take time to regain control. She excused herself to the living room. I followed her, continuing to talk. She excused herself and went upstairs to our bedroom. Yes, you guessed it! I followed her to the bedroom, talking now with increased energy. Luella excused herself to the bathroom and once again I followed her. She looked at me with a bit of a smile and said, "You don't get it, do you? I am trying to get away from you so that we don't sin any more than we already have. Please don't follow me. We both need time to think, pray, and gain control before we can have a productive talk." At that point I decided to quit following her. She was right in reminding me that as a child of God, self-control is a choice. We must not forget the power of the indwelling Spirit or ignore the damage that is done when we do not exercise the control we have in him.

I have seen how long the sting of hurtful words lingers. I have learned to confess that I am not free from struggles with impatience, selfishness, and pride. For me, and for some of you, this temptation to let words fly in moments of anger will remain to some extent until Christ returns. Again and again I need to say to myself, "No! Stop! Wait. Pray. Think. Speak," exercising the self-control I have been given in Christ.

The opposite tendency is to *clam up*. Some of us find *flight* much more natural and comfortable than *fight*. Some of you tend to hold onto your anger. You tend to stew and replay the videotape of a hurtful scene over and over in your mental VCR, getting more angry and bitter with each repetition. Some of you are very skilled at punishing others with your silence. You, too, have given way to the passions and desires of the sinful nature. You, too, have failed to exercise the self-control that is yours in Christ. You need to resist the urge to run away. You need to stay on the scene. You need to speak loving words of truth to your neighbor. You need to say, "No! Stop! Wait. Pray. Think. Speak," before you give in to the temptation to run away.

To you, Paul would say, "Don't ever let the sun set on your anger." I mentioned earlier that one marriage-saving commitment Luella and I made early in our relationship was that we would not go to sleep while we were still unreconciled. This commitment led to some rather humorous bedroom scenes early in our marriage. We would both be angry and too proud to ask for forgiveness, yet very aware of the commitment we had made. We would lie in bed, trying to stay awake while we waited for the other person to give in and admit that he or she was wrong! Sometimes we would almost have to physically hold our eyes open before one of us would say, "Are you still awake? I am very sorry that. . . ."

As we remained faithful to this commitment, we began to learn the value of keeping short accounts. Today moments of conflict in our relationship are very short-lived. Usually within a few minutes, one of us is seeking forgiveness. Because we are dealing with problems while they are still small, solutions come more easily. But when we allow negative emotions to grow and grow, we give the Devil an opportunity to do his work.

What is the Devil's work? It is deception, division, and destruction. He lurks, waiting to seize any opportunity to turn our anger into something more destructive and deadly. He works to change our anger into a grudge, into poisonous bitterness, into a stubborn refusal to forgive, and into ugly thoughts of vengeance. He nurtures these seeds into thorns of broken relationships, defensiveness, cynicism, and doubt. So, Paul says, "Be aware of the work of the Devil before you speak your first word. Settle matters quickly. Don't give him any ground on which to stand. Do everything you can to thwart his work."

Does the way we handle our anger give room for the Devil? What is our tendency? Is it to *blow up* or to *clam up*? What changes do we need to make in the way we deal with anger? What kinds of things make us angry? What do they reveal about the true treasures of our hearts? Has a "created thing" become more important than the Creator (Rom. 1:25)?

Praise God for the empowering presence of the Holy Spirit (Eph. 3:14–20)! Because of him, we can exercise control over things that once controlled us.

Choosing Words of Grace

Perhaps this is the highest goal for talk within the body of Christ—that our words would be conduits of the life-giving grace of the Lord Jesus Christ. Here we really do focus on being part of what God is doing in the lives of others. Here we die to the hopes, dreams, and desires of self so that his purposes may reign. Here we view our relationships from the vantage point of *ambassadors*. What does this mean? It means recognizing that our relationships do not belong to us. People do not exist for our happiness and contentment; rather, God has appointed us to faithfully communicate his powerful love for them. (See chapter 7 for a detailed discussion of 2 Cor. 5:11–21.)

Let's look at Paul's words as he calls us to talk in a way that gives grace.

> *Do not let any unwholesome talk come out of your mouths, but only what is helpful for building others up according to their needs, that it may benefit those who listen. And do not grieve the Holy Spirit of God, with whom you were sealed for the day of redemption. (Eph. 4:29–30)*

Paul emphasizes five elements of grace-full talk.

1. *Be unshakably committed to wholesome talk.* When Paul says, "Forbid any unwholesome talk from entering your conversa-

tion," he is not just talking about cursing, swearing, or vulgar, four-letter words. In fact, to think of the passage this way grossly minimizes its intent. Paul has something much more redemptively revolutionary in mind. For Paul, unwholesome talk is *me-centered* talk that has no higher purpose than my own wants, desires, dreams, and demands. Unwholesome words flow from a heart that is controlled by present, personal, earthly desire. They are spoken because they please *me* and accomplish my goals. They are an attempt to get me what I want, without reference to the lordship of Christ or my call to speak as his ambassador.

I have counseled many husbands and wives in sadly broken marriages who would never have gotten to that point had they simply heeded this principle. If me-centered, my-desire communication had been replaced early with ambassadorial talk (What is important to the Lord here, and how can I speak in a way that promotes it?), their marriages would never have reached the tragic point of disintegration.

Each of us needs to face how powerful the war of desire is in our hearts—how easy it is to have our words shaped by no higher purpose than our own pleasure. We need to recognize how often we speak as if we were totally unaware of the Lord, his work, and his call to be instruments of his grace.

What, then, is wholesome talk? It is *other-oriented* communication that is rooted in the existence, love, mercy, grace, and calling of the Lord. It submits to his plan, speaks up to his standard, and uses words unselfishly. It finds meaning and joy in being used by God as he works in others.

Wholesome talk is also other-oriented in the way it has the needs of others as its focus. Words are specifically spoken for the benefit of those who listen. Wholesome talk flows from a heart that loves God above all else and one's neighbor as oneself. We will never talk this way if our hearts are filled with our own desires, goals, demands, and needs.

Only when we entrust ourselves into the Lord's sovereign care are we free to speak this way. In our own selfishness, doubt, and fear, we want to take control with our talk, making sure we get the things our hearts are set upon. ("I need his respect." "I've just gotta have this job!" "She has to know how much she hurt me!" "I'll teach him to respect me if it is the last thing I do!" "If I don't win this argument, things will only get worse." "I'll have to handle her with kid gloves." "I've got to show him that this is not the first time he did this to me.") Wholesome talk submits both to the call of God and the need of our neighbor.

2. *Consider the person to whom you are talking* (". . . only what is helpful for building others up"). As we saw in chapter 12, Paul is saying something revolutionary here: we should only speak things that consider how our listeners need to be built up.

To whom we are speaking? Is it a man, woman, boy, or girl? Is it someone our own age, younger, or older? Is it a long-time friend, a casual acquaintance, or a virtual stranger? Is it a family member, a distant relative, or a neighbor? Is the person a believer, a seeker, or lost? What is his or her knowledge and experience of the truths of Scripture? How receptive is this person to my ministry? How do the answers to these questions guide me in what to say?

3. *Consider the problem you are being called to address* (". . . for building others up according to their needs"). To consider the problem means to ask, What is the need of the moment? What gift of grace is needed? How can I speak as an instrument of that grace?

Is there some specific sin that needs to be lovingly confronted? Is the work of peacemaking needed because there is disunity and division? Is there spiritual blindness? A loss of hope? Are there pockets of doubt about God? Is there the confusion of many counselors and conflicting advice? Is there fear, anxiety, and dread? Is there anger, malice, bitterness, and vengeance? Is there a lack of biblical knowledge, wisdom, and insight? Are there patterns of direct rebellion against God? Is there selfishness, pride, or self-righteousness that needs to be faced? Is there an unwillingness to accept responsibility? Is there a need for thanksgiving, praise, and worship?

Having the right agenda makes a critical difference in communication. So often parents, for example, enter the rooms of their children with a *punitive* rather than a *ministry* agenda. They do little more than point out wrong (usually infected with their own anger and hurt) and announce punishment. They neglect to ask the essential question, that is, What does God want to do in the heart of my child through me? Attention to this principle alone would result in radical changes in our relationships!

4. *Consider the process* (". . . that it may benefit [give grace to] those who listen"). Paul says it this way in Colossians 4:6: "Let your conversation be always full of grace, seasoned with salt, so that you may know how to answer everyone." God's goal for our communication is grace; that is, that our words would be of specific spiritual benefit to those who hear. This is not just a "don't do" passage, but more powerfully a "do" passage. God does not want us to stand wimpishly by, in fear that we would say the wrong thing. No, we are called to exercise the courage of faith, to think and speak decisively as agents of the King who rules every relationship and every situation. We must always keep the unseen world of spiritual realities in view and talk in a way that produces a harvest of spiritual fruit in those who hear us.

When we have focused on God's goal of grace (spiritual benefit), we need to ask what the best way is to reach it. What is the best way, the best place, and the best time to say what needs to be said so that this person will benefit as God has planned?

Permit me to use the parental example again. Often parents lecture their children in an attempt to get them to see the wrong they have done. The problem is that this is the wrong process. As the parents are lecturing, the child is doing two things: (1) silently defending, excusing, and arguing in his mind, and (2) anxiously waiting for the "conversation" to be over. Perhaps you've even heard your child say at the end of one of your lectures, "Are you done yet?" These are not exactly words of repentance! If I have prepared myself by considering the best process of communication, I will enter the room knowing that what my teenager needs is the grace of conviction and confession. I want to speak to my child in a way that would lead him to confession. Perhaps this means it is better to ask open-ended questions that enable the child to examine the situation, his thoughts and motives, and his behavior than it is to tell him what I think. I don't just want him to agree with me; I want him to see himself accurately in the mirror of the Word of God. I do not want him to do business with me, but with God.

In every situation I need to ask, What is the best way for my words to accomplish God's goal of grace? This answer will be different according to the situations and the people involved.

5. *Don't let your speech hinder the Holy Spirit's work.* ("And do not grieve the Holy Spirit of God, with whom you were sealed for the day of redemption.") What is the primary work of the Holy Spirit? To make us holy. This progressive, life-long work of sanctification is ongoing in every situation and relationship. He *is* working in "all things" for our good, so that we would be conformed to the image of the Son (Rom. 8:28–30). It is a terrible thing when our selfish, unwholesome talk gets in the way!

This is why Paul reminds us that God sealed us for the day of redemption. A seal is a sign of ownership. From the moment of our new birth, we no longer belong to ourselves. Neither do our words. Paul repeats this principle in 1 Corinthians 6:19: "Do you not know that your body is a temple of the Holy Spirit, who is in you, whom you have received from God? You are not your own; you were brought at a price.

Therefore honor God with your body." And, I would add, with your talk.

God is saying, "I own you and I have chosen you to be part of my work of holiness in the lives of others. Don't get in the way!" To avoid this, we need to completely rid our talk of bitterness, rage, anger, brawling, slander, and malice. These are all evidences of a heart controlled by personal desires and demands, of a heart that has taken ownership of our lives away from God. When we act this way, we need to remember that we have already been bought and sealed by God.

Choosing Words of Forgiveness

There is no call of Christ more difficult than the call to forgive others as he has forgiven us. Paul says:

> Be kind and compassionate to one another, forgiving each other, just as in Christ God forgave you. Be imitators of God, therefore, as dearly loved children and live a life of love, just as Christ loved us and gave himself up for us as a fragrant offering and sacrifice to God. (Eph. 4:32–5:2)

Words of forgiveness involve several things.

1. *Greet the sin of others with* judicial *forgiveness.* Judicial forgiveness is a step of heart preparation. I covenant with God to let go of the offense the person has committed against me and entrust him or her to the Lord's work of conviction and justice. Peter says of Christ, "When they hurled their insults at him, he did not retaliate; when he suffered, he made no threats. Instead, he entrusted himself to him who judges justly" (1 Peter 2:23). Christ did not retaliate (verbally or otherwise) because he had a lively and practical trust in his Father. This teaches me that forgiving the people who have sinned against me is always the fruit of faith in God. Trust in

God moves my heart from thoughts of vengeance to thoughts of reconciliation, from plans of judgment to purposes of love. All this prepares me for the next step of forgiveness.

2. *Greet the sin of others with* relational *forgiveness.* Relational forgiveness differs from judicial forgiveness in that it cannot be offered until the person asks for it. The problem for many of us is that because we have not dealt with the heart issue of judicial forgiveness, we are completely unprepared to offer relational forgiveness when someone comes seeking it. We are still angry and harboring thoughts of vengeance. The last thing we want to do is forgive the person we think needs to be punished.

These two aspects of forgiveness are so important in the Christian life! Sinners will surround us until we leave this world. There will seldom be a day when we are not sinned against in some way. From the flesh wound of another's thoughtlessness to the deep, stabbing wounds of horrible abuse, sinners sin against one another. But there is another thing that is true. Sinners tend to respond sinfully to being sinned against. This is why forgiveness is so vitally important. It is not just for the other person, but for our good as well. Otherwise, our hearts will be controlled by anger, bitterness, and vengeance, giving the Devil an opportunity to do his cruel work.

Scripture is clear that it makes no sense to rejoice in the amazing forgiveness we have received in Christ if we refuse to forgive others (see Matt. 18:21–35). Scripture is clear that committing myself to forgive means being willing to do it over and over again—maybe even several times a day with the same person (see Luke 17:1–6)! Finally, God's Word stresses that forgiveness should not be taken for granted, but that we must *speak* unmistakable words of forgiveness to one another. Our model of forgiveness is the Lord, who does not assume that we will understand that he has forgiven us. He declares it over and over again in his Word. Relational forgiveness always means *speaking* words of forgiveness to the offender.

It is not helpful to say "That's okay" or "It's no problem"

to a person who has been convicted of sin by the Holy Spirit and has come to seek forgiveness. The Lord already has convinced the person that what he did was *not* okay. He needs the gift of forgiveness from you to put his heart at rest. In this situation, we need to say, "I forgive you and I have already committed myself never to bring this issue up to myself, to you, or to others." These words do two things: they block the work of the enemy and they promote the work of sanctification and reconciliation that the Holy Spirit has already begun.

Our failure to speak clear words of forgiveness to someone who has wronged us may be the most common way we hinder the Spirit's work and give the Devil an opportunity. Words of forgiveness do more than just heal human relationships; they promote God's work of conforming us to Christ.

3. *Greet the sin of others with words of blessing.* To forgive doesn't mean that I am willing once again to barely tolerate your presence in my life. Forgiveness is active. It replaces hatred with love. It replaces malice with compassion, bitterness with joy, desires for vengeance with desires for blessing. When the Lord forgives, he doesn't merely tolerate us back into fellowship with him. No, he showers us with his blessing. He offers us new mercies every morning. He fills our cup to overflowing! Genuine words of forgiveness will always lead to words of blessing.

Here, once more, we are called to follow the example of the Lord. God does not only accept us into his family, but as he lovingly works in us and through us, he *motivates* us with lovingly and liberally spoken words of blessing. *He* blesses us with words that caress our souls like salve on a wound. When we are wronged, we need to look for opportunities to speak words of blessing to one another. These are words of love, comfort, grace, patience, gentleness, and kindness, words of peace and encouragement. They pour water on the fires of anger. They are used by God to quiet the storms of conflict. They submit to his call to bless those who have mistreated us, who have done evil to us (Luke 6:27). They recognize that we defeat evil not by making war with the passions and desires of the sinful nature, but by overcoming evil with good in action and words (Rom. 12:9–21). They bring us to our knees as we admit, once again, that only in the Lord's strength can we speak this way. Consider how many opportunities we have given the enemy by responding to the sins of others with irritation, impatience, accusations, and threats. No wonder we are unprepared to respond in a godly manner when more serious offenses are laid at our feet!

This was the case with Shirley and Jim. When Jim committed one act of sexual unfaithfulness, Shirley did everything she could to hurt him. She called everyone she could think of to damage his reputation. She sought to destroy any respect their children may have had for him. Why did Shirley respond this way? Why was she unprepared to deal with Jim's offense in a godly way? In this moment of major crisis, Shirley was simply doing what she had always done with the small offenses of daily life. In these situations, Shirley seldom responded with words of forgiveness and blessing. Instead she looked for the most hurtful thing she could say to Jim. She held onto the offense, and she shared all of Jim's lesser sins with anyone who was around.

Perhaps we are talking about the "faithful in little, faithful in much" principle. Minor offenses are God's training ground for us, so that we can learn to deal with sin God's way. Then we will be prepared to do and say what is right when a major offense comes. Our words will promote the work of the Spirit and give no room for the Devil to do his deceitful, destructive work.

World of Evil or Tool for Good?

We've come to the end of our consideration of the great war of words. It began with a lie in the Garden and it still rages on. The damage can be seen in our offices, kitchens, family rooms, and cars, but the battle isn't really fought there. Battles of the tongue are really battles of the heart. What controls the heart will control the tongue. The tongue can set "the whole course of life on fire," or it can be used to "give grace to the ones who hear." It can viciously tear down or lovingly build up. It can condemn or give life. It can greet sin with love and forgiveness or with hatred and revenge. It can submit to the lordship of Christ or live under the control of the passions and desires of the sinful nature. It can pursue a lifestyle of ministry or a lifestyle of self-love, manipulating others to meet personal desires and expectations. It can be a fount of truth or a polluted stream of falsehood. It can create peace or cause war. It can curse or it can praise.

In it all, the tongue will serve the master to which the heart is already committed. It is time for us to submit to the Lord's claim on our tongues as our King and Redeemer. More than ever before, we need to be committed to speak for him.

As we do, we will learn to choose words of truth, love, restraint, grace, and forgiveness, even in the face of provocation. We will get excited about the grandeur of our calling as children of God. It is amazing that God would choose us to be members of his family! It is beyond amazing that he would call us to be his ambassadors, to represent him on earth, to communicate his loving appeal to a world enslaved to self.

The war of words is only won when God rules our hearts so that we gladly and consistently speak for him. May God help us, so that this world of evil will be transformed into a world of redemptive good. May he win the war for our hearts so that the battleground of words becomes a garden of good fruit, where the seeds of peace produce a lasting harvest of righteousness (James 3:18).

Getting Personal:
A Final Assessment

1. As you have read this book, what have you learned about the thoughts and motives of your heart?

2. What have you learned about your communication struggles? (marital, parental, friendship, family, body of Christ, etc.)
3. Where is God calling you to repentance?
Put off:

Put on:

4. What specific opportunities is God giving you to be part of what he is doing in the lives of others?
5. What promises of the gospel encourage you as you answer God's call to change?

■　■　■　■　■

Paul Tripp is president of Paul Tripp Ministries, a nonprofit organization whose mission statement is "Connecting the transforming power of Jesus Christ to everyday life." This mission leads Paul to weekly speaking engagements around the world. From 2007 to 2011, Paul was also on the pastoral staff at Tenth Presbyterian Church in Philadelphia, Pennsylvania, where he preached on Sunday evenings and led the Ministry to Center City. Paul is also the Professor of Pastoral Life and Care at Redeemer Seminary in Dallas, Texas, and the Executive Director of the Center for Pastoral Life and Care in Fort Worth, Texas, and has taught at respected institutions worldwide. Paul has written ten books on Christian living that are read and distributed internationally. He has been married for many years to Luella, and they have four grown children. For speaking engagements and other information, see www.paultrippministries.org.

RESOURCES FOR CHANGING LIVES BOOKLETS

A.D.D.: Wandering Minds and Wired Bodies, by Edward T. Welch
Anger: Escaping the Maze, by David Powlison
Angry at God? Bring Him Your Doubts and Questions, by Robert D. Jones
Bad Memories: Getting Past your Past, by Robert D. Jones
Depression: The Way Up When You Are Down, by Edward T. Welch
Domestic Abuse: How to Help, by David Powlison, Paul David Tripp, and Edward T. Welch
Forgiveness: "I Just Can't Forgive Myself!" by Robert D. Jones
God's Love: Better than Unconditional, by David Powlison
Guidance: Have I Missed God's Best? by James C. Petty
Homosexuality: Speaking the Truth in Love, by Edward T. Welch
"Just One More": When Desires Don't Take No for an Answer, by Edward T. Welch
Marriage: Whose Dream? by Paul David Tripp
Motives: "Why Do I Do the Things I Do?" by Edward T. Welch
OCD: Freedom for the Obsessive-Compulsive, by Michael R. Emlet
Pornography: Slaying the Dragon, by David Powlison
Pre-Engagement: 5 Questions to Ask Yourselves, by David Powlison and John Yenchko
Priorities: Mastering Time Management, by James C. Petty
Procrastination: First Steps to Change, by Walter Henegar
Self-Injury: When Pain Feels Good, by Edward T. Welch
Sexual Sin: Combatting the Drifting and Cheating, by Jeffrey S. Black
Stress: Peace Amid Pressure, by David Powlison
Suffering: Eternity Makes a Difference, by Paul David Tripp
Suicide: Understanding and Intervening by Jeffrey S. Black
Teens and Sex: How Should We Teach Them? by Paul David Tripp
Thankfulness: Even When It Hurts, by Susan Lutz
Why Me? Comfort for the Victimized by David Powlison
Worry: Pursuing a Better Path to Peace, by David Powlison

FOR FURTHER INFORMATION

Speaking engagements with authors in this series may be arranged by calling The Christian Counseling and Educational Foundation at (215) 884-7676.

Videotapes and audio cassettes by authors in this series may be ordered through Resources for Changing Lives at (800) 318-2186.

For a complete catalog of titles from P&R Publishing, call (800) 631-0094.